NORMAND DALLAIRE

The
FOUR
GOSPELS
Into One Book

According To
Matthew, Mark, Luke, John
with no
'If' or 'But'

I am the Rock

I am the Bread of Life

I am the Living Water

I am the Door

NORMAND DALLAIRE

The
FOUR
GOSPELS
Into One Book

According To
Matthew, Mark, Luke, John
with no
'If' or 'But'

I am the Rock

I am the Bread of Life

I am the Living Water

I am the Door

ARPress
ILLUMINATING IDEAS.
EMPOWERING VOICES

ARPress
45 Dan Road Suite 5
Canton MA 02021

| Hotline: | 1(888) 821-0229 |
| Fax: | 1(508) 545-7580 |

Ordering Information:

Quantity sales. Special discounts are available on quantity purchases by corporations, associations, and others. For details, contact the publisher at the address above.

Printed in the United States of America.

ISBN-13:	Softcover	979-8-89330-454-1
	eBook	979-8-89330-455-8
	Hardback	979-8-89330-456-5

Library of Congress Control Number: 2024901211

Table of Contents

Preface

Most of religious people and born-again Christians knows that, when you read the same story in two or three Gospel's we have sometime three different versions, the witness they do not agree with each other and sometime there is no witnesses. The question is why they are so discrepancies between each other Gospel's. So, we have to "wonder" "Why?"??

\# 1 Where were they when they wrote their Gospel?

\# 2 How old were they?

\# 3 Where are the witness, who witnesses all?

\# 4 Who did the translation of their Gospel?

Let's look at the first question.

\# 1 Where were they? Most likely they were hiding from religious persecutions. The religious machine operated by Jewish people didn't believe that Jesus was their Savior and the Christ. And they had to hide away from city dwelling, they had to be far away from main roads, and maybe live in the mountain where you can find cavern and such.

\# 2 How were they? They were around 80 to 90 years old when they wrote it. And this is 50 to 60 years after the fact.

\# 3 Where are their witnesses, after 50 to 60 years after the resurrection. Most likely, decease after so long after the resurrection.

\# 4 Who did the translation, are they worthy?

It is not easy to translate one language to another. You will find some language barrier, and some are harder to crack than some others.

Do they Apostles who wrote these Gospel lie---- to us, lets find out. These authors were in their ninety maybe. Now their witnesses are gone, and they heard each individual story one by one, specially when they never witness themselves. and they heard, and heard, and heard these story so many times by different people who heard them from mouth to mouth and after 50 to 60 years later, you are telling a certain story and you believe that you were there when it happened, and you were not there.

So, your brain play "trick" on you after all those years, only because you getting older. Of course, its not universal and every senior citizen got it after approaching that age. So, did they lie, I will say a definitely---NO.

Now I will tell you who did put lies, and lies in the Bible, and most likely in the New Testament, and its loaded.

James VI and I (James Charles Stuart June 19/1566 TO March 27/1625) Was King of Scotland as James VI and King of England and Ireland as James I in 1603.

James, coronation as King of England, a conference of churchmen, (religious church) requested that the "English Bible" be revised because existing translations, was corrupt and not answerable to the truth of the "original" (Word of God) and contain several inconsistencies. And, in 1604 the project started. They had more than 50 theologians, scholars from many denominations' churches and many different religious churches. And they want to make sure that they had their saying in that New Bible.

So now tell me as smart as you might be do you think that this "Good Book" will be after all their bickering about whose right, that when the finish product is done, that this New Bible will be A GOOD BOOK. It can't because too many different "organizations" are involved, I am talking when human factors also, it cannot come out right. With too many doctrines you can't make every body happy. And the New Testament was hit very hard because of Jesus of His life and resurrection. And everyone wanted a piece of that, and tell it the way they see it fit to their own doctrine.

And in all of these, theologians and scholars they were a big bunch who were very bad theologians and also some very bad scholars. I was not there to see it, today I know what they did. God contradict Himself in the Bible Jesus did lie at least four time. And it is impossible four God to lie, and in the Bible He did. Oh, I completely forgot, its not God who wrote the Bible, its men. And God did say that every man, is a liar.

And I will do something about that. (almost) Every Bible today from different denominations and religious churches take their origin from the King James Bible. I give myself three years, and I will re- write a New testament with no discrepancies, no lies, and no mistakes in it. Let's change subject, ok.

What is actually a 24hr. day according to God. In Genesis 1:3-5. God say, "Let there be light"; and there was light. And God saw the light, that it was good; and God divided the light from the darkness. God called the light Day, and the darkness He called Night. So, the evening and the morning were the first day. Sunset to Sunset. God also want it more holiday for us and Him, that we should be together.

In Leviticus 23: v.15 He started a new holiday, the Feast of Weeks. This is very important for us to know that Feast of Weeks because, it will happen when the year that Jesus will go to calvary, it will be that "Special Sabbath" year that year. Every 50years. A week for God is 7 years, so, 7x7=49 and the year after is the year that the Passover Sabbath will not be on a Saturday that year, for instance the year that Jesus will do His last Passover will be a Thursday. He will die on wed: at 3pm. And 3hr. later it was the Passover. And it will be the beginning of Thursday new day. Don't forget it is sunset to sunset a 24hr. day for Him.

Jesus was crucified on "Preparation Day" it is the day before the Passover, so it was Wednesday, and He die that Wednesday at 3pm. Jesus Himself said that He will be 3 days(12x3-36hr.) and 3-night (12x3=36hr.) 36+36=72hr. That is 3 full days.

And Jesus said He will be 3 (full) days in the heart of the earth.

Jesus died wed:3pm. And at 5.59.59pm He had to be buried by that time according to the Jewish Law.

Wednesday 6pm to Thursday 6pm is the first full day.

Thursday 6pm to Friday 6pm is the second full day.

Friday 6pm to Saturday 6pm is the third full day that Jesus is in the ground. At 6pm Saturday it is a new day who just started and it is Sunday. This is why that Jesus did not resurrect the third day, it was on the fourth day. In Matthew it said in ch:28. Now after the Sabbath (after the Passover) as the first day of the week begin to dawn, etch.

I hope you understand this clearly that Jesus did not resurrect <u>on</u> the third day, He was resurrected the fourth day. The first day of the week, is always a Sunday.

Happy reading.

DEDICATION

To all my brothers and sisters in the Lord, who are "Wondering" can we believe everything that is in the Bible. Well personally I do not believe what the Bible say.

Per-say? I believe what God say in the bible. And there is some instance that I know that God did not say it this way, God do not make mistakes. I dedicate this book to all those who did teach me with their writing for many books I read. Thank you for this treasure of information I pick it up over the years,

I will like to thanks my good friend <u>Josee Moisan</u> for all her help, its because of her that I can reach you. May God <u>continue</u> to bless all of you x7.

CHAPTER 1

1 The Eternal Word

¹In the beginning was the Word, and the Word was with God, and the Word was God. ² He was in the beginning with God. ³ All things were made through Him, and without Him nothing was made that was made. ⁴ In Him was life, and the life was the Light of men. ⁵ And the light shines in the darkness, and the darkness did not comprehend it.

2 The genealogy of Jesus Christ

⁶ God created Adam, and Adam begot Seth by Eve and was the mother of all living. ⁷ Seth begot Enosh, Enosh begot Cainan, ⁸ Cainan begot Mahalalel, Mahalalel begot Jared, Jared begot Enoch, ⁹ Enoch begot Methuselah, Methuselah begot Lamech, Lamech begot Noah, ¹⁰ Noah begot Shem, Shem begot Arphaxad, Arphaxad begot Cainan, ¹¹ Cainan begot Shelan, Shelan begot Eber, Eber begot Peleg, ¹² Peleg begot Reu, Reu begot Serug, Serug begot Nahor, ¹³ Nahor begot Terah, Terah begot Abram(ham), Abram begot Isaac, ¹⁴ Isaac begot Jacob, Jacob begot Judah, Judah begot Perez, ¹⁵ Perez begot Hezron, Hezron begot Ram, Ram begot Amminadab, ¹⁶ Amminadab begot Nashon, Nashon begot Salmon, Salmon begot Boaz, ¹⁷ Boaz begot Obed, Obed begot Jesse, Jesse begot David, ¹⁸ David begot Nathan, Nathan begot Mattatha, Mattatha begot Menan, ¹⁹ Menan begot Melea, Melea begot Eliakim, Eliakim begot Jonan, ²⁰ Jonan begot Joseph, Joseph begot Judah, Judah begot Simeon, ²¹ Simeon begot Levi, Levi begot Mattathias, Mattathias begot Jorim, ²² Jorim begot Eliezer, Eliezer begot Jose, Jose begot Er, ²³ Er begot Elmodam, Elmodam begot Cosam, Cosam begot Addi, ²⁴ Addi begot Melchi, Melchi begot Nerie,

Nerie begot Shealtiel, ²⁵ Shealtiel begot Zerubbabel, Zerubbabel begot Rhesa, Rhesa begot Joanna's, ²⁶ Joanna's begot Judah, Judah begot Joseph, Joseph begot Semei, ²⁷ Semei begot Mattathiah, Mattathiah begot Maath, Maath begot Nagai, ²⁸ Nagai begot Esli, Esli begot Nahum, Nahum begot Amos, ²⁹ Amos begot Mattathiah, Mattathiah begot joseph, Joseph begot Janna, ³⁰ Janna begot Melchi, Melchi begot Levi, Levi begot Matthat, ³¹ Matthat begot Heli, Heli begot Joseph, the husband of Mary of whom was born Jesus who is called Christ. ³² Jesus Christ the Son of David, the Son of Abraham.

3 Luke dedication to Theophilus

³³ In as much as many have taken in hand to set in order a narrative of those things which have been fulfilled among us, ³⁴ just as those who from the beginning were eye witnesses and ministers of the Word delivered them to us, ³⁵ it seems good to me also having had perfect understanding of all things, from the very first, to write to you an orderly account, most excellent Theophilus, ³⁶ that you may know the certainty of those things in which you were instructed.

4 John Birth Announced to Zachariah

³⁷ There was in the days of Herod, the King of Judea, a certain Priest named Zacharias, of the division of Abijah. His wife was of the daughter of Aaron, and her name was Elizabeth. ³⁸ And they were both righteous before God. Walking in all the commandments and ordinances of the Lord blameless. ³⁹ Only they had no child, because Elizabeth was barren, and they were both well advanced in years. ⁴⁰ So it was, that while he was serving as Priest before God in the order of his division, ⁴¹ according to the custom of the Priesthood, his lot fell to burn incense when he went to the Temple of the Lord. ⁴² And the whole multitude of the people was praying outside at the hour of incense. ⁴³ Then an Angel of the Lord appeared to him, standing on the right side of the Altar of the incense. ⁴⁴ And when Zacharias saw him, he was troubled, and fear fell upon him.

⁴⁵ And the Angel said to him, "Do not be afraid, Zacharias, for your prayer is heard; and your wife Elizabeth will bear a son, and you should call his name John. ⁴⁶ And you will have joy and gladness, and many will rejoice at his birth. ⁴⁷ For he will be great in the sight of the Lord

and shall drink neither wine nor strong drink. He will also be filled with the Holy Spirit, even from his mother's womb. [48] And he will turn many of the children of Israel to the Lord their God. [49] He will also go before Him in the spirit and power of Elijah, to turn the hearts of the fathers to the children, and the disobedient to the wisdom of the just, to make ready a people prepared to the Lord." [50] And Zacharias said to the Angel, "How shall I know this? For I am an old man, and my wife is well advanced in years."

[51] And the Angel answered and said to him, "I am Gabriel, who stands in the presence of God, and was sent to speak to you and bring you these glad tidings. [52] Pay attention, you will be mute and not be able to speak until the day these things take place, because you did not believe my words which will be fulfilled in their own time." [53] And the people waited for Zacharias, and marveled that he lingered so long in the Temple. [54] Only when he came out, he could not speak to them; and perceived that he had a vision in the Temple, for he beckoned to them and remained speechless.

[55] So it was, as soon as the days of his service were completed, that he departed to his own house. [56] Now after those days his wife Elizabeth conceived; and she hid herself the fifth months, saying, [57] "thus the Lord has dealt with me" in the days when He looked on me, to take away my reproach among people".

5 Christ's birth announced to Mary

[58] Now in the six month the Angel Gabriel was sent by God to a city of Galilee named Nazareth, [59] to a virgin betrothed to a man whose name was Joseph, of the house of David. The virgin's name was Mary. [60] And having come in, the Angel said to her, "Rejoice, highly favored one, the Lord is with you; blessed are you". [61] And when she saw him, she was troubled at his saying, and considered what manner of greeting this was. [62] Then the Angel said to her, "do not be afraid, Mary, for you have found favor with God. [63] And Behold, you will conceive in your womb and bring forth a Son, and shall call His Name Jesus.

[64] He will be great and will be called the Son of the Highest; and the Lord will give Him the throne of His father David. [65] And He will reign over the house of Jacob forever, and of His Kingdom there will

be no end". [66] Then Mary said to the Angel, "How can this be, since I do not know a man"? [67] And the Angel answered and said to her. And the Angel departed from her.

6 Mary visited Elizabeth

[71] Now Mary arose in those days and went into the hill country with haste, to a city of Judah, [72] and entered the house of Zacharias and greeted Elizabeth. [73] And it happened, when Elizabeth heard the greeting of Mary, that the baby leaped in her womb; and Elizabeth was filled with the Holy Spirit. [74] Then she spoke out with a loud voice and said, "Blessed are you among women, and blessed is the fruit of your womb! [75] And why is this granted to me, that the mother of my Lord should come to me? [76] For indeed, as soon as the voice of your greeting sounded in my ears, the baby leaped in my womb with joy. [77] Blessed is she who believed, for there will be a fulfillment of those things which were told her from The Lord."

CHAPTER 2

1 The song of Mary

[1] And Mary said: "My soul magnifies the Lord, and my spirit has rejoiced in God my Savior."

[2] "For He has regarded the lowly state of His maidservant; for behold, henceforth all generations will call me blessed. [3] For He who Is mighty has done great things for me, and holy is His Name. [4] And His mercy is on those who fear Him from generation to generation. He has shown strength with His arm; He has scattered the proud and the imagination of their hearts. [5] He has put down the mighty from their thrones and exalted the lowly. [6] He has filled the hungry with good things, and the rich He sent away empty. [7] He has helped His servant Israel, In remembrance of His mercy, as He spoke to our fathers, to Abraham and to His seed forever." [8] And Mary remained with her about three months and returned to her house.

2 Birth of John (the Baptist)

[9] Now Elizabeth full time came for her to be delivered, and she brought forth a son. [10] When her neighbors and relatives heard how the Lord had shown great mercy to her, they rejoiced with her.

3 Circumcision of John

[11] So it was, on the eight days, that they came to circumcise the child; and they would have call him by the name of his father, Zacharias. [12] His mother answered and said, "No; he shall be called John". [13] They say to her, there is no one among your relatives who is called by this name.

[14] So, they ask the father what he would have him called. [15] And he asked for a writing tablet, and wrote saying, "His name is John". And they marveled. [16] Immediately his mouth was opened, and his tongue loosed, and he spoke, praising God. [17] Then fear came on all who dealt around them; and all these saying were discussed throughout all the hill country of Judea. [18] And all those who heard them kept them in their hearts, saying, "what kind of child will this be". And the hand of the Lord was with him.

4 Zacharia's Prophecy

[19] Now his father Zacharias was filled with the Holy Spirit, and prophesied, saying:

[20] Blessed Is the Lord God of Israel, for He has visited and redeemed His people, [21] and has raised up a horn of salvation for us in the house of His servant David, as He spoke by the mouth of His holy Prophets. Who have been since the world began, [23] that we should be saved from our enemies and from the hand of all who hate us, [24] to perform the mercy promised to our fathers and to remember His holy covenant, [25] The oat which He swore to our father Abraham; [26] to grant us that we, being delivered from the hand of our enemies, might serve Him without fear, [27] in holiness and righteousness before Him all the days of our life.

[28] And you, child, will be called the Prophet of the Highest; for you will go before the face of the Lord to prepare His ways, [29] to give knowledge of salvation to His people by the remission of their sins, [30] through the tender mercy of our God, with which the Dayspring from on high has visit us; [31] to give light to those who sit in darkness and the shadow of death, to guide our feet into the way of peace.

[32] So, the child grew and became strong in spirit and was in the desert till the day of his manifestation to Israel.

5 Christ born of Mary

[33] And it came to pass in those days that a decree went out from Caesar Augustus that all the world should be registered. [34] This census, took, place while Quirinius was Governing Syria. [35] And all went to be registered, everyone to his own city. [36] Now the birth of Jesus Christ was as follows; after His mother Mary was betrothed to Joseph, they came

together, she was found with Child of the Holy Spirit. [37] Then Joseph, being a just man, and not wanting to make her a public example, was minded to put her away secretly. [38] And while he thought about these things, Behold, an Angel of the Lord appeared to him in a dream, saying, "Joseph, son of David, do not be afraid to take to you Mary to be your wife, for that which is conceived in her is of the Holy Spirit. [39] And she will bring a Son, and you shall call His Name Jesus, for He will save His people from their sins".

[40] Joseph also went up from Galilee, out of the city of Nazareth, into Judea, to the city of David which he called Bethlehem, because he was of the lineage of David, [41] to be registered with Mary, his future wife, who was with child. [42] Then Joseph, being aroused from sleep, did as the Angel of the Lord commanded him and to took to him his wife, [43] and did not know her till she had brought forth a Son, and wrapped Him in swaddling, cloths, and laid Him in a manger, because they were no room for them in the Inn. [44] And all this was done that it might be fulfilled which was spoken by the Lord through the Prophet Isaiah, saying, [45] Behold, the virgin shall be with child, and bear a Son, and they shall call His name Immanuel, which is translated, "God with us."

6 Glory in the Highest

[46] Now there were in the same country shepherds living out in the fields, keeping watch over their flock by night. [47] And an Angel of the Lord stood before them, and the glory of the Lord shone around them, and they were greatly afraid. [48] Then the Angel said to them, "Do not be afraid, for Behold, I bring you good tidings of great joy which will be to all people. [49] For there is born to you this day in the city of David a Savior Who is Christ the Lord.

[50] And this will be the sign to you: "You will find a Babe wrapped in swaddling cloths, lying in a manger". [51] And suddenly there was with the Angel a multitude of the heavenly host praising God and saying: [52] Glory to God in the Highest, and on earth peace, toward men of goodwill.

[53] And it was, when the Angels had gone away from them into Heaven, that the shepherds said to one another, "Let us now go to Bethlehem and see this thing that has come to pass, Which the Lord

has made known to us". [54] And they came with haste and found Mary and Joseph, and the Babe lying in a manger. [55] Now when they had seen Him, they made known the saying which was told them concerning this Child. [56] And all those who heard it marveled at those things which were told them by the shepherds.

[57] And Mary kept all these things and pondered them in her heart. [58] Then the shepherds returned, glorifying and praising God for all things that they had heard and seen, as it was told them.

CHAPTER 3

1 Circumcision of Jesus

[1] And when eight days were completed for His circumcision, His name was called Jesus, the name given by the Angel before he was conceived in the womb.

Jesus presented in the Temple.

[2] As it was written in the Law of the Lord, "Consecrate to Me all the first born, whatever opens the womb among the children of Israel, both of men and beast; it is Mine". [3] Now when the days of her purification according to the Law of Moses were completed, they brought Him to Jerusalem to present Him to the Lord, [4] and to offer a sacrifice according to what is said in the Law of the Lord, "A pair of turtledoves or two young pigeons".

2 Simeon see's God's Salvation

[5] And Behold, there was a man in Jerusalem whose name was Simeon, and this man was just and devout, waiting for the consolation of Israel, and the Holy Spirit was upon him. [6] And it had been revealed to him by the Holy Spirit that he would not see death before he had seen the Lord Jesus Christ. [7] So he came by the Spirit into the Temple,

And when the parents brought in the Child Jesus, to do for Him according to the custom of the law, [8] he took Him up in his arms and blessed God and said:

[9] "Lord, now you are letting your servant depart in peace, according to your word; [10] for my eyes have seen Your salvation, "which You have prepared before the face of the people, [12] a Light to bring revelation

to the Gentiles, and the glory of Your People Israel". And his father (adoptive) and mother marveled at those things which were spoken of Him. [14] Then Simeon blessed them, and said to Mary His mother, "Behold, this Child is destined for the fall and rising of many in Israel, and for a sign which will be spoken against [15] (Yes, a sword will pierce through your own soul also), that the thoughts of many hearts will be revealed".

3 Anna bear witness to The Redeemer

[16] Now there was one, Anna a Prophetess, the daughter of Phanuel, of the tribe of Asher. She was of a great age and had lived with a husband seven years from her virginity; [17] and this woman was a widow until she was eight-four, who did not depart from the Temple, and served God with fasting and prayers night and day. [18] And coming in that instant she gives thanks to God, and spoke of Him to all those who looked for redemption in Jerusalem.

4 Wise Men from the East

[19] Now after Jesus was born in Bethlehem of Judea in the days of Herod the King, Behold, wise men from the East came to Jerusalem, [20] saying, "Where is He who has been born King of the Jews? For we have seen His Star in the East and have come to worship Him."

[21] When Herod the King heard this, he was troubled, and all Jerusalem with him. (The Priesthood also) [22] And when he gathered all the Chief Priests and Scribes of the people together, he inquired of them where the Christ was to be born.

[23] And they said to him, "In Bethlehem of Judea, for thus it is written by the Prophet MICAH: [24] And you Bethlehem, in the land of Judah, are not the least among the rulers of Judah; for out of you should come a Ruler Who will Shepherd My people Israel".

[25] Then Herod, when he had secretly called the wise men, determined from them what time the Star appeared. [26] And he sent them to Bethlehem and said, "Go and search carefully for the young Child, (Jesus was about 1 year and half at that time) and when you have found Him, bring back word to me, that I may come and worship Him also".

²⁷ When they heard the King, they departed; and Behold, the Star that they had seen in the East went before them, till it came and stood over where the young Child was. ²⁸ When they saw the Star, they rejoiced with exceedingly great joy. ²⁹ And when they had come into the house, they saw the young Child with Mary His mother, and fell down and worshiped Him. And when they had opened their treasures, they presented gifts to Him; gold, frankincense and myrrh.

³⁰ Then, being divinely warned in a dream that they should not return to Herod, they departed, for their own country another way.

5 The flight into Egypt

³¹ Now when they departed, Behold, an Angel of the Lord appeared to Joseph in a dream, saying, "Arise, take the young Child and His mother, flee to Egypt, and stay there until I bring you Word; for Herod will seek the young Child to destroy Him".

³² When he arose, he took the young Child and His mother by night and departed for Egypt, ³³ and was there until the death of Herod, that it might be fulfilled which was spoken by the Lord through the Prophet Hosea, saying, "Out of Egypt I call My Son".

6 Massacre of the innocents

³⁴ Then Herod, when he saw that he was deceived by the wise men, was exceedingly angry; and he went forth and put to death all the male children who were in Bethlehem and in all its districts, from two years old and under, according to the time which he had determined from the wise men. ³⁵ Then was fulfilled what was spoken by Jeremiah the Prophet, saying: ³⁶ "A voice was heard in Ramah, lamentation, weeping and great mourning, Rachel weeping for her children, refusing to be comforted, because they are no more".

7 The family return to Nazareth

³⁷ Now when Herod was dead, Behold, an Angel of the Lord appeared in a dream to Joseph in Egypt, ³⁸ saying, "Arise, take the young Child and His mother, and go to the land Of Israel, for those who sought the young Child's life are dead". ³⁹ Then he arose, took the young Child and His mother, and came into the land of Israel.

[40] And when he heard that Archelaus was reigning over Judea instead of his father Herod, he was afraid to go there. And being warned by God in a dream, he turned aside into the region of Galilee. [41] And he came and dwelt in a city called Nazareth, that it might be fulfilled which was spoken by the Prophets, "He shall be called a Nazarene". [42] And the Child grew and became strong and filled with wisdom; and the grace of God was upon Him.

8 The Boy Jesus amazes the Scholars

[43] His parents went to Jerusalem every year at the feast of the Passover. [44] And when He was twelve years old, they went up to Jerusalem according to the custom of the feast. [45] When they had finished the days, as they returned, the Boy Jesus lingered behind in Jerusalem. And His parents did not know it; [46] and supposing Him to have been in the company, they went a day's journey, and sought Him among their relatives and acquaintances. [47] So when they did not find Him, they returned to Jerusalem, seeking Him.

[48] Now so it was that after three days they found Him in the Temple, sitting in the midst of the teachers, both listening to them and asking them questions. [49] And all who heard Him were astonished at His understanding of the Word of God and answers. [50] So when they saw Him, they were amazed; and His mother said to Him, "Son why have You done this to us? Look, your father and I have sought You anxiously". [51] And He said to them, "Why did you seek Me? Did you not know that I must be about My Father's business"? And they did not understand the statement which He spoke to them.

9 John witness, the True Light

[52] There was a man sent from God, whose name was John. [53] This man came for a witness, to bear witness of the Light, that all through Him might believe. [54] He was not that Light and was sent to bear witness to that Light. [55] That was the True Light which gives light to every man coming into the world. [56] He was in the world, and the world was made through Him, and the world did not know Him. [57] He Came to His Own and His own did not receive Him. [58] And as many as received Him, to them He gave the right to become Children of God, to those who believe in His Name: [59] who were born, not of blood, nor of the will of the flesh, nor of the will of man, only of God.

10 The Word became flesh

[60] And the Word became flesh and dwelt among us, and we beheld His glory, The glory as of the only begotten of the Father, full of grace and truth.

[61] John bare witness of Him and cried out, saying, "This was He of Whom I said, "He Who came after me is preferred before me, for He was before me". [62] For of His fulness we have all received, and grace for grace."

[63] For the Law was given through Moses, and grace and truth came through Jesus Christ, [64] No one has seen God at anytime. The only begotten God, Who is in the bosom of the Father, He has declared Him.

11 John the Baptist prepares the Way

[65] Now in the fifteenth year of the reign of Tiberius Caesar, Pontius Pilato being Governor of Judea, Herod being tetrarch of Galilee, his brother Philip tetrarch Abilene, [66] in the high priesthood of Annas and Caiaphas, The Word of God came to John the son of Zacharias in the wilderness. [67] And saying, "Repent, for the kingdom of Heaven is at hand! [68] For this is He Who was spoken of by the Prophet Isaiah, [69] saying: "The voice of one crying in the wilderness: "Prepare the way of the Lord; make His path straight."

[70] Now John himself was clothed in camel's hair with a leather belt around his waist; and his food was locusts and wild honey. [71] Then Jerusalem, all Judea, and all the region around the Jordan went out to him [72] and were Baptized by him in the Jordan, confessing their sins.

[73] And when he saw many of the Pharisees and Sadducees coming in the Baptism, he said to them, "Brood of vipers! Who warned you to flee from the wrath to come? [74] Therefore bear fruit worthy of repentance, [75] and do not think to say to yourselves, we have Abraham as our father; for I say to you that God is able to raise up children to Abraham from these stones. [76] And even now the axe is laid to the root of the trees. Therefore, every tree which does not bear good fruit is cut down and thrown into the fire. [77] I indeed Baptize you with water into repentance, and He Who is coming after me is mighty than I, whose sandals I am not worthy to carry.

He will Baptize you with the Holy Spirit. [78] His winnowing fan is in His hand, and He will thoroughly clean out His threshing floor, and gather His wheat into the barn; and He will burn the chaff with unquenchable fire".

CHAPTER 4

1 A voice in the wilderness

¹ Now this is the testimony of John, when the Jews sent Priest and Levites from Jerusalem to ask him, "Who are you?" ² He confessed and did not deny. Only confessed, "I am not the Christ." ³ And they ask him, "What then? Are you Elijah?" He said, "I am not." Are you the Prophet? And he answered, "No."

⁴ They said to him, "Who are you, that we may give an answer to those who sent us? What do you say about yourself?" ⁵ He said: The Prophet Isaiah did say "I am the voice of one crying in the wilderness: Make straight the way of the Lord."

⁶ Now those who were sent were from the Pharisees. ⁷ And they asked him, saying, "Why then do you Baptize with water, when you are not the Christ, nor Elijah, nor the Prophet?" ⁸ John answered them, saying, "I Baptize with water, and there stands One Whom you do not know.

⁹ It is He Who coming after me, is preferred before me, whose sandal strap I am not worthy to lose." ¹⁰ These things were done in Bethany beyond the Jordan, where John was Baptizing.

2 John preaches to the people

¹¹ Then he said to the multitudes that came out to be Baptized by him, "He who has two tunics, let him give to him who has none; and he who has food, let him do likewise."

¹² Then tax collectors also came to be Baptized, and said to him, "teacher what shall we do?" ¹³ And he said to them, "collect no more than what is appointed for you." ¹⁴ Likewise the soldiers ask him, saying,

"And what shall we do?" And he said to them, "Do not intimidate anyone or accuse falsely, and be content with your wages."

[15] Now as the people were in expectation and all reasoned in their heart about John, whether he was the Christ or not.

3 John Baptize Jesus

[16] I did not know Him, only He Who sent me to Baptize with water said to me, "Upon Whom you see the Spirit descending, and remaining on Him, this is He Who Baptize with the Holy Spirit.

[17] Then Jesus came from Galilee to John at the Jordan to be Baptized by him. [18] And John tries to prevent Him, saying, "I need to be Baptized by You, and You are coming to me?"

[19] And Jesus answered to him, "Permit it to be so now, for thus it is fitting for us to fulfill all righteousness." Then he allows Him.

[20] When He had been Baptized Jesus came up immediately from the water; and Behold, the Heavens were opened to Him, and I John saw the Spirit descending from Heaven like a Dove, and He remained upon Him. [21] And suddenly a voice came from Heaven, saying, "This Is My beloved Son, in Whom I am well pleased." [22] And I have seen and testified that this is the Son of God.

4 Satan tempts Jesus

[23] Then Jesus, being filled with the Holy Spirit, returned from the Jordan and was let by the Spirit in the wilderness, [24] being tempted for forty days and forty nights by the devil, and in those days, He ate nothing and afterward, when they had ended, He was hungry.

[25] And the devil says to Him "Supposing You are the Son of God, command this stone to become bread." [26] And Jesus Him saying, "It is written, man shall not live by bread alone, only by every Word of God."

[27] "Then the devil, taking Him up on a high mountain, showed Him all the kingdoms of the world in a moment of time. [28] And their glory; for this has been delivered to me, and I give it to whomever I wish. [29] Therefore, supposing You will worship before me, all will be Yours."

[30] And Jesus answered and said to him, "It is written, you shall worship the Lord your God, and Him only you shall serve."

[31] Then he brought Him to Jerusalem, set Him on the pinnacle of the Temple, and said to Him, "Supposing You are the Son of God, throw Yourself down from here. [32] For it is written: 'He shall give His Angels charge over You, to keep You'. [33] And, 'in their hands they shall bear You up, lest You dash Your foot against a stone." [34] And Jesus answered and said to him, "It has been said, you shall not tempt the Lord your God."

[35] Now when the devil has ended every temptation, he departed from Him until an opportune time. [36] And Angels came and ministered to Him.

5 Jesus rejected at Nazareth

[37] So He came to Nazareth, where He had been brought up. And as His custom was, He went into the Synagogue on the Sabbath day, and stood up to read. [38] And He was handed the book of the Prophet Isaiah. And when He had opened the book, He found the place where it was written:

[39] *"The Spirit of the Lord is upon Me, because He has anointed Me to preach the Gospel to the poor; He has sent Me to heal the broken-hearted, to proclaim liberty to the captives and recovery of sight to the blind, to set at liberty those who are oppressed; [40] to proclaim the acceptable year of the Lord."*

[41] The He closed the book, and gave it back to the attendant and sat down. And the eyes of all who were in the Synagogue were fixed on Him. [42] And He began to say to them, "Today this Scripture is fulfilled in your hearing." [43] So all bore witness to Him, and marveled at the gracious words which proceeded out of His mouth. And they say, "Is this not Joseph's Son?" [44] He said to them, "You will surely say this proverb to Me, 'Physician, heal yourself! Whatever we have heard done in Capharnaum, do also here in Your country'."

[45] Then He said, "Assuredly, I say to you, no Prophet is accepted in his own country. [46] And I tell you truly," many widows were in Israel in the days of Elijah, when the Heaven was shut up to three and six months, and there was a great famine throughout all the land; [47]

and none of them was Elijah sent except to Zarephath, in the region of Sidon, to a woman who was a widow. [48] And many lepers were in Israel in the time of Elijah the Prophet, and none of them was cleansed except Naaman the Syrian."

[49] So all these in the Synagogue, when they heard these things, were filled with wrath, [50] and rose up and thrust Him out of the city; and let Him to the bow of the hill on which their city was build, that they might through Him down over the cliff. [51] Then passing through the midst of them, He went His way.

6 Jesus began His Galilean ministry

[52] Now when Jesus heard that John had been put in prison, He departed to Galilee. [53] And leaving Nazareth, He came and dwelt in Capharnaum, which is by the sea, in the regions of Zelalem and Naphtali, that it might be fulfilled which was spoken by Isaiah the Prophet, saying: [54] The land of Zelalem and the land of Naphtali, by the way of the sea, beyond the Jordan, Galilee of the Gentiles; [55] the people who sat in darkness have seen a Great Light, and upon those who sat in the region and shadow of death Light has dawned.

[56] Now when it was day, He departed and went into a deserted place. And the crowd sought and come to Him and try to keep Him from leaving them; [57] and He said to them, "I must Preach the Kingdom of God to the other cities also, because of this purpose I have been sent." [58] From that time Jesus began to Preach and to say, "Repent, for the Kingdom of Heaven is at hand."

CHAPTER 5

1 The first Disciples

[1] So it was, as the multitude pressed about Him to hear The Word of God, that He stood by the lake of Gennesaret, [2] and saw two boats standing by the lake; and the fishermen had gone from them and were washing their nets. [3] Then He got into one of the boats, which was Simon's, and asked him to put out a little from the land. And He sat down and taught' the multitude from the boat.

[4] When He had stopped speaking, He said to Simon, "Launch out into the deep and let down your nets for a catch." [5] And Simon answered to Him, "Master, we have tailed all night and caught nothing; nevertheless, at Your Word I will let down the net."

[6] And when they had done this, they caught a great number of fish, and their net was breaking. [7] So they signaled to their partners in the other boat to come and help them. And they came and filled both the boats, so that they begin to sink. [8] When Simon Peter saw it, he fell down at Jesus knees, saying, "Depart from me, for I am a sinful man, O Lord!"

[9] For he and all who were with him were astonished at the catch of fish which they had taken; [10] and so also were James and John, the sons of Zebedee, who were partners with Simon. And Jesus said to Simon, "Do not be afraid. From now on you will catch men." [11] Now when Jesus looked at him, He said, "You are Simon the son of Jonah. You shall be called Cephas" (which is translated a stone).

2 Philip and Nathaniel

[12] The following day Jesus wanted to go to Galilee, and He found Philip and said to him, "Follow Me." [13] Now Philip was from Bethsaida

(Bethany), the city of Andrew and Peter. [14] Philip found Nathaniel and said to him, "We have found Him of Whom Moses in the Law, and also the Prophets, wrote-Jesus of Nazareth, the Son of Joseph."

[15] And Nathaniel said to him, "Can anything good came out of Nazareth?" Philip said to him, "Come and see."

[16] Jesus saw Nathaniel coming towards Him, and said to him, "Behold, an Israelite indeed, in whom is no deceit!"

[17] Nathaniel said to Him, "How do you know me?" Jesus answered and said to him, "Before Philip called you, when you were under the fig tree, I saw you."

[18] Nathaniel answered and said to Him, "Rabbi You are the Son of God! You are the King of Israel!"

[19] Jesus answered and said to him, "Because I said to you, I saw you under the fig tree," do you believe? You will see greater things than these." [20] And He said to him, "Most assuredly, I say to you, you shall see Heaven open, and the Angels of God ascending and descending upon the Son of Man."

3 Matthew tax collector

[21] As Jesus passed on from there, He saw a man named Matthew sitting at the tax office. And said to him, "Follow me", and he arose and follow Him. [22] Now it happened, as Jesus sat at the table in the house, that Behold, many tax collectors and sinners came and sat down with Him and His Disciples. [23] And when the Pharisees saw it, they said to His Disciples, "Why does your teachers eat with tax collectors and sinners?"

[24] When Jesus heard that, He said to them, "Those who are well have no need of a physician, only those who are sick." [25] You go and learn what it means: "I desire mercy and not sacrifice. For I did not come to call the righteous, only sinners." (Hosea 6:6)

4 The twelve Apostles

[26] Now it come to pass in those days that He went out to the mountain to pray and continue all night in prayer to God.

[27] And when it was day, He called His Disciples to Himself; and far from them He chose twelve whom He also named Apostles: [28] Now the names of the twelve Apostles are these: First, Simon, who is called Peter, and Andrew his brother James the son of Zebedee, and John his brother, [29] Philip and Bartholomew, Thomas and Matthew the tax collector, James the son of Alphaeus, and Thaddeus, Simon the Canaanite (Cananaean) and Judas Iscariot, who also betrayed Him.

5 Jesus cleans the Temple

[30] Now the Passover of the Jews was at hand, and Jesus went up to Jerusalem. [31] And He found in the Temple those who sold oxen and sheep and doves, and the money changes doing business, [32] when He had made a whip of cords, He drove them all out of the Temple, with the sheep and the oxen, and poured out the change's money and overturned the tables. [33] And He said to those who sold doves, "It is written, "For My house shall be called a house of prayer for all nation" (Isaiah 56: 7) and you have made it a "den of thieves" (Jeremiah 7: 11)

[34] Then the blind and the lame came to Him in the Temple, and He healed them. [35] And when the Chief Priests and Scribes saw the wonderful things that He did, and the children crying out in the Temple and saying, "HOSANNA to the Son of David!" They were indignant

[36] and said to Him, "Do You hear what these are saying?" And Jesus said to them, "Yes, have you never read, (Ps.8:2) out of the mouth of babes and nursing infants you have perfected strength?" [37] And the Jews said, "What sign do You show to us, since You do these things? [38] "Then Jesus answered and said to them, "destroy this Temple, and after three days I will raise it up."

[39] Then the Jews said "It has taken forty-six years to build this Temple, and will You raise it up after three days?" [40] And the Scribes and Chief-Priests heard it and sought how they might destroy Him; for they fear Him, because all the people were astonished at His Teaching. [41] Then He left them and went out of the city to Bethany, and He lodged there.

6 The Bread from Heaven

[42] On the following day, when the people who were standing on the other side of the sea saw that they were no other boat there, except one, and that Jesus had not entered the boat with His Disciples, and His Disciples had gone away alone [43] however, other boats came down from Tiberias, near the place where they ate bread after the Lord had given thanks [44] when the people therefore saw that Jesus was not there, nor His Disciples they also got into boats and came to Capharnaum, seeking Jesus.

[45] And when they found Him on the other side of the sea, they said to Him, "Rabbi, when did You came here?" [46] Jesus answered them and said, "Most assuredly, I say to you, you seek Me, not because you saw the signs, only because you ate of the loaves and were filled. [47] Do not labor for the food which perishes, only for the food which endures to Everlasting Life, which the Son of Man will give you, because God the Father has set His seal on it."

[48] They said to Him, "What shall we do, that we may work the works of God?" [49] Jesus answered and said to them, "this is the work of God that you believe In Him Whom He sent." [50] Therefore they said to Him, "What sign will You perform then, that we may see it and believe You? [51] Our fathers ate the manna in the desert; as it is written, He gave them bread from Heaven to eat. (Nehemiah 9:15) [52] Then Jesus said to them, "Most assuredly, I say to you, Moses did not give you the bread from Heaven. [53] Only My Father gives you the True Bread from Heaven. [54] For the Bread of God is He Who comes down from Heaven and gives Life to the world." [55] Then they said to Him, "Lord, give us this Bread always."

[56] And Jesus said to them, "I Am the Bread of Life. He/she who comes to Me shall never hunger, and he/she who believes in Me shall never thirst. [57] And I said to you that you had seen Me and yet do not believe. [58] All that the Father gives Me will come to Me, and the one who come to Me, I will by no means cast out. [59] For I have come down from Heaven, not to do My own will, only the will of Him Who sent Me.

[60] This is the will of the Father Who sent Me, that of all He has given Me I should lose nothing, and should raise it up at the last day.

[61] And this is the will of Him Who sent Me, that everyone who sees the Son and believes In Him may have Everlasting Life; and I will raise him/her up at the last day.

CHAPTER 6

<u>1 Rejected by His own</u>

[1] The Jews then complained about Him, because He said, "I Am the Bread which came down from Heaven." [2] And they said, "Is not this Jesus, the Son of Joseph, whose father and mother we know? How is it then that He says, "I have come down from Heaven." [3] Jesus therefore answered and said to them, "Do not murmur among yourselves. [4] No one can come to Me unless the Father Who sent Me will draws him / her; and I will raise him/her up at the last day.

[5] It is written by the Prophets, "And they shall be Taught by God. Therefore, everyone who has heard and learned from the Father comes to Me. [6] Not that anyone has see the Father, except He Who is from God; He has seen the Father. [7] Most assuredly, I say to you, he/she believes in Me has Everlasting Life. [8] I am the Bread of Life. [9] Your fathers ate the manna in the wilderness, and are dead. [10] This is the Bread which came down from Heaven, that one may eat of it and not die. [11] I am the Living Bread which came down from Heaven. When anyone eats of this Bread, he/she will live forever; and the Bread that I shall give is My flesh, which I shall give for the life of the world."

[12] The Jews therefore quarreled among themselves, saying, "How can this Man give us His flesh to eat?" [13] Then Jesus said to them, "Most assuredly, I say to you, unless you eat the flesh of the Son of Man and drink His blood, you have no life in you. [14] Whoever eats My flesh and drink My blood has Eternal Life, and I will raise him/her up at the last day. [15] For My flesh is food indeed, and My blood is drink indeed. [16] He/She who eats My flesh and drink My blood abides in Me, and I in him/her. [17] As the Living Father sent Me, and I live because of the Father, so he/she who feed on Me will live because of Me. [18] This is

the Bread which came down from Heaven---not as your fathers ate the manna, and are dead. He/she who eats this Bread will live forever." [19] These things He said in the Synagogue as He Taught in Capharnaum.

2 Jesus healed a great multitude

[20] And Jesus went about all Galilee, Teaching in their Synagogues, Preaching the Gospel of the Kingdom, and healing all kinds of sickness and all kinds of disease among the people. [21] Then His fame went throughout all Syria; and they brought to Him all sick people who were afflicted with various disease and torments, and those who were demon-possessed, epileptics; and paralytics; and He healed them.

[22] Great multitudes follow Him—from Galilee, and from Decapolis, Jerusalem, Judea, and beyond the Jordan. [23] And the whole multitude sought to touch Him, for POWER went out from Him and healed them all.

3 Beatitudes

[24] And seeking the multitudes, He went up on a mountain, and when He was seated His Disciples came to Him. [25] Then He open His mouth and Taught them saying:

[26] Blessed are the poor in spirit, for theirs is the Kingdom of Heaven.

[27] Blessed are those who mourn, for they shall be comforted.

[28] Blessed are the meek, for they shall inherit the earth.

[29] Blessed are those who hunger and thirst for righteousness for they shall be filled.

[30] Blessed are the merciful, for they shall obtain Mercy.

[31] Blessed are the pure heart for they shall see God.

[32] Blessed are the peacemakers, for they shall be called sons of God.

[33] Blessed are those who are persecuted for righteousness' sake for theirs is the Kingdom of Heaven.

[34] Blessed are you when they revile and persecuted you, and say all kinds of evil against you falsely for My sake.

³⁵ Rejoice and be exceedingly glad, for great is your reward in Heaven, for so they persecuted the Prophets who were before you.

4 Water turned in wine

³⁶ On the third day there was a wedding in Cana of Galilee, and the mother of Jesus was there. ³⁷ Now both Jesus and His Apostles were invited to the wedding. ³⁸ And they ran out of wine, the mother of Jesus said to Him, "They have no wine."

³⁹ Jesus said to her, "woman what does your concern have to do with Me? My hour has not yet come." ⁴⁰ His mother said to the servants, "whatever He says to you, do it." ⁴¹ Now there were set there six waterpots of stone, according to the manner of purification of the Jews, containing twenty or thirty gallons a piece. ⁴² Jesus said to them, "Fill the waterpots with water." And they filled them up to the brim.

⁴³ And He said to them, "Draw some out now, and take it to the master of the feast." And they took it. ⁴⁴ When the master of the feast had tasted the water that was made wine, and did not know where it came from, (the servants who had drawn the water knew) the master of the feast called the bridegroom, ⁴⁵ and said to him, "Every man / woman at the beginning sets out the good wine, and when the guests have well drunk, then the inferior. You have kept the good wine until now!"

⁴⁶ This beginning of signs Jesus did in Cana of Galilee, and manifested His glory; and His Apostles believed in Him. ⁴⁷ After this He went down to Capharnaum, He, His mother, His brothers, and His Apostles; and they did not stay there many days.

5 The discerner of hearts

⁴⁸ Now when He was in Jerusalem at the Passover, during the feast, many believed in His Name when they saw the signs which He did. ⁴⁹ Only Jesus did noy commit Himself to them, because He knew all men, ⁵⁰ and had no need that anyone should testify of man (everyone), for He knew what was in the men hearts.

6 Adultery in the heart

⁵¹ You have heard that it was said, "You shall not commit adultery." And I say to you that whoever looks at a woman/man to lust for her/

him has already committed adultery with her/him in his/her heart. [52] When your right eye causes you to sin, pluck it out and cast it from you; for it is more profitable for you that one member perished than for your whole body to be cast into hell. [53] And when your right hand causes you to sin, cut it off and cast it from you; for it is more profitable for you that one of your members perish, than for your whole body to be cast in hell.

CHAPTER 7

1 Believers are Salt and Light

¹ Salt is good. You are the Salt of the earth; and when the salt loses its flavor, how shall it be seasoned? It is good for nothing and to be thrown out and trembled underfoot by men. ² It is neither fit for the land nor for the dunghill, and men throw it out? ³ You are the Light of the world. A city that is set on a hill cannot be hidden. ⁴ Nor do they light a lamp and put it under a basket, you put it on the lampstand, and it gives light to all who are in the house. ⁵ Let your Light so shine before men, that they may see your good works and glorify your Father in Heaven.

2 Christ fulfill the Law

⁶ Do not think that I came to destroy the Law or the Prophets. I did not come to destroy only to fulfill. ⁷ For assuredly, I say to you, till Heaven and earth pass away, one jot or one tittle will by no means pass from the Law till all is fulfilled.

⁸ Wherever therefore breaks one of the least of these commandments, and teaches men so, shall be called least in the Kingdom of Heaven, and whoever does and teaches them, he/she be called great in the Kingdom of Heaven. ⁹ For I say to you, that unless your righteousness exceeds the righteousness of the Scribes and, Pharisees you will by no means enter the kingdom of Heaven.

3 Jesus cast out an unclean spirit

¹⁰ Then they went in Capharnaum, and immediately on the Sabbath He entered the Synagogue and Taught. ¹¹ And they were astonished at

His Teaching, for He Taught them as One having Authority, and not as a Scribes.

¹² Now there was a man in their Synagogue with an unclean spirit. And he cried out, ¹³ saying, "Let us alone! What have we to do with You, Jesus of Nazareth? Did You come to destroy us? I know who You are—THE HOLY ONE OF GOD?" ¹⁴ And Jesus rebuke him, saying," Be quiet, and come out of him!" ¹⁵ And when the unclean spirit had convulsed him and cried out with a loud voice, he came out of him. ¹⁶ Then they were all amazed, so that they questioned among themselves, saying, "What is this? What new doctrine is this? For with authority, He commands even the unclean spirits, and they obey Him." ¹⁷ And immediately His fame spread throughout all the region around Galilee.

4 Murder begins in the heart

¹⁸ "You have heard that it was said to these of old." "You shall not murder, (Exodus 20:13) and whoever murders will be in the danger of the judgment. ¹⁹ And I say to you that whoever is angry with his/her brother, or sister shall be of the danger of the judgment. And whoever says to his/her brother or sister "RACA" shall be in danger of the council. And whoever says" YOU FOOL" shall be in danger of the hell fire.

²⁰ Therefore when you bring your gift to the Altar, and there remember that your brother or sister has something against you, ²¹ leave your gift there before the Altar, and go your way. First be reconciled to your brother or sister and then come and offer your gift.

²² Agree with your adversary quickly, while you are on the way with him/her, lest your adversary will deliver you to the judge, the judge hand you over to the officer, and you be thrown into prison. ²³ Assuredly, I say to you, you will by no means get out of there till you have paid the last penny.

5 Marriage is Sacred and Binding

²⁴ Now it came to pass, when Jesus had finished these saying, that He departed from Galilee and came to the region of Judea beyond the Jordan. ²⁵ And great multitudes followed Him, and He healed them there.²⁶ The Pharisees also came to Him, testing Him, and saying to

Him, "Is it lawful for a man or a woman to divorce his or her spouse for just any reason?"

²⁷ And He answered and said to them, "Have you not read that He Who created them at the beginning made them male and female, (Genesis 1:27), (and to become one, man has to do it and do what God say)" ²⁸ and, "For this reason men will leave his father and mother and be joined to his wife, and the two should become one flesh? (Genesis 2:24)"

²⁹ And then, they are no longer two, only, "one flesh." Therefore, what God has joined together let not man or woman separate."

³⁰ They said to Him, "Why then did Moses's command to give a certificate of divorce, and to put his or her away?" ³¹ He said to them, "Moses, because of the hardness of your hearts permitted you to divorce your spouse, and from the beginning it was not so. ³² And I say to you whoever divorces his or her spouse, except for sexual immorality and marries another, commit adultery; and whoever marries him or her who is divorced commits adultery."

³³ His Disciples said to Him, when such is the case of the man with his wife, it is better not to marry? (did you see, Jesus didn't answer his question, maybe it was a stupid question to begin with)

6 Peter's mother- in- law healed

³⁴ Now He arose from the Synagogue and entered Simon's house. And Simon's wife mother was sick with a high fever, and they made request of Him concerning her. ³⁵ So He stood over her and rebuke the fever, and it left her. And immediately she arose and serve them.

CHAPTER 8

1 Jesus healed a leper

[1] Now a leper came to Him, imploring Him, kneeling down to Him and saying to Him, "Lord, when You are willing, You, can make me clean." [2] Then Jesus, moved with compassion, stretched out His hand and touched him, and said to him, "I am willing; be cleansed." [3] As soon as He had spoken, immediately the leprosy left him, and he was cleansed. [4] And He strictly warned him to tell no one. And go and show yourself to the Priest, and make an offering for your cleansing, as a testimony to them, just as Moses commanded.

[5] However, he went out and began to proclaim it freely, and to spread the matter, so that Jesus could no longer openly enter the city, only, was outside in deserted places; and they came to Him from every direction.

2 Jesus is questioned about fasting

[6] The disciples of John and of the Pharisees were fasting. Then they came and said to Him, "Why do the disciples of john and of the Pharisees fast, only Your Disciples do not fast?" [7] And He said to them, "Can you make the friends of the bridegroom, fast while the bridegroom is with them? And the days will come when the bridegroom will be taken away from them; then they will fast in those days."

[8] Then He spoke a parable to them: No one puts a piece from a new garment on an old one; otherwise, the new makes a tear, and also the piece that was taken out of the new does not match the old. [9] And no one puts new wine into old wineskins; or else the new wine will burst the wineskins and be spilled, and the wineskins will be ruined. [10] Only new wine must be put into new wineskins, and both are preserved. [11]

And no one, having drunk old wine, desires new; for he says, "The old is better."

3 The new birth

[12] There was a man of the Pharisees named Nicodemus, a ruler of the Jews. [13] This man came to Jesus by night and said to Him, "Rabbi, we know that You are a Teacher come from God; for no one can do these signs that You do unless God is with Him." [14] Jesus answered and said to him, "Most assuredly, I say to you, unless one is born-again, he/she cannot see the Kingdom of God." [15] Nicodemus said to Him, "How can a man /woman be born when he/she old? Can he/she enter a second time into his/her mother's womb and be re-born?"

[16] Jesus answered, "Most assuredly, I say to you, unless one is born of water and the Spirit, he/she cannot enter the Kingdom of God. [17] That which is born of the flesh is flesh, and that which is born of the Spirit is spirit. [18] Do not marvel that I said to you, "You must be born-again." [19] The wind blow where it wishes, and you hear the sound of it, and cannot tell where it comes from and where it goes. So is everyone who is born of the Spirit." [20] Nicodemus answered and said to him, "How can these things be."

[21] Jesus answered, and said to him, "Are you the teacher of Israel, and do not know these things? [22] Most assuredly, I say to you, we speak what we know and testify what we have seen, and you do not receive our witness. [23] And I have told you earthly things and you do not believe; how will you believe when I tell you Heavenly things? [24] No one has ascended to Heaven except He who came down from Heaven, that is the Son of Man.

[25] And as Moses lifted up the serpent in the wilderness, even so must the Son of Man be lifted up, [26] that whoever believes in Him should have Eternal Life. [27] For God so loved the world that He gave His only begotten Son, that whoever believes in Him should not perish, except to have Eternal Life. [28] For God did not send His Son into the world to condemn the world, and that the world through Him might be saved.

[29] He/She who believes in Him is not condemned; except he/she who do not believe is condemned already, because he/she has not believed in the Name of the only begotten Son of God. [30] and this is the

condemnation, that the Light has come into the world, and men loved darkness rather than Light, because their deeds were evil.

[31] For everyone practicing evil hates the Light and does not come to the Light, lest his /her deeds should be exposed. [32] And he/she who does the truth comes to the Light, that is deed may be clearly seen, that they have been done in God."

4 Jesus forbids oats

[33] Again you have heard that it was said to those of old, "You should not swear falsely, except, shall perform your oats to the Lord."

[34] Only I say to you, do not swear at all: neither by Heaven, for it is God's throne, [35] nor by the earth, for it is His footstool, nor by Jerusalem, for it is the city of the great king. [36] Nor shall you swear by your head, because you cannot make one hair white or black. [37] Only let your YES be YES and your NO, be NO. For whatever is more than these is from the evil one.

5 Go the second mile

[38] You have heard that it was said, "An eye for an eye and a tooth for a tooth (Exodus 21:24). [39] And I tell you not to resist an evil person. And whoever slaps you on your right cheek, turn the other to him/her also. [40] When anyone wants to sue you and take away your tunic, let him/her have your cloak also. [41] And whoever compels you to do one mile, go with him/her two. [42] Give to him/her who ask you, and from him/her who wants to borrow from you do not turn away.

6 Love your enemies

[43] And I say to you who hear: Love your enemies, do good to those who hate you. [44] Bless those who curse you, and pray for those who spiffily use you. And when you love those who love you, what credit is that to you? For even sinners love those who love them. [45] And you do good to those who do good to you, what credit is that to you? For even sinners do the same. [46] And when you lend to those from whom you hope to receive back, what credit is that to you? For even sinners lends to sinners to receive as much back.

[47] And love your enemies, Do good and lend, hoping for nothing in return; and your reward will be great, and you will be the sons and daughters of the Most High. For He is kind to the unthankful and evil. [48] Therefore be merciful, just as your Father also is merciful. [49] And when you greet your brother/sister, only, do you do more than others? Do not, even the tax collectors do so? [50] Therefore you shall be perfect, just as your Father in Heaven is perfect.

7 The rich man and Lazarus

[51] There was a certain rich man who was clothed in purple and fine linen and fared sumptuously every day. [52] And there was a certain beggar named Lazarus, full of sores, who was laid at his gate, [53] desiring to be fed with the crumbs which fell from the rich man table. Moreover, the dogs came and licked his sores. [54] So it was that the beggar died, and was carried by the Angels to Abraham's bosom. The rich man also died and was buried. [55] And being in torments in Hades, he lifted up his eyes and saw Abraham afar off, and Lazarus in his bosom.

[56] Then he cried and said, "Father Abraham, have mercy on me, and send Lazarus that he may dip the tip of his finger in water and cool my tongue; for I am tormented in this flame: [57] And Abraham said, "Son, remember that in your lifetime you received your good things, and likewise Lazarus evil things; and now he is comforted and you are tormented. [58] And besides all this, between us and you there is a great gulf fixed, so that those who want to pass from here to you cannot, nor can those from there pass to us!

[59] The he said, "I beg you therefore, father, that you would send him to my father's house, [60] for I have five brothers, that he may testify to them, lest they also come to this place of torment: [61] Abraham said to him, "They have Moses and the Prophets; let them hear them:" [62] And he said, "No, father Abraham; only when one goes to them from the dead, they will repent:" [63] And he said to him, "Except they do not hear Moses and the Prophets, neither will they be persuaded though one rise from the dead."

CHAPTER 9

1 Many healed after Sabbath sunset

[1] When the sun was setting, all those who had any that were sick with various diseases brought to Him, and He laid His hands on every one of them and healed them. [2] And demons also came out of many, crying out and saying, YOU ARE THE SON OF GOD, and He rebuke them, and did not allow them to speak, for they knew that He was the Christ.

2 Jesus is the Lord of the Sabbath

[3] Now it happened that He went through the grainfields on the Sabbath; and as they went His Apostles began to pluck the heads of grains. [4] And the Pharisees said to Him, "Look, why do they do what is not lawful on the Sabbath?" [5] And He said to them, "Have you ever read what David did when he was in need and hungry, he and those with him; [6] how he went into the house of God in the days of Abiathar the High Priest, and ate the Showbread, which is not lawful to eat except for the Priests, and also gave some to those who were with him."

[7] And He said to them, "The Sabbath was made for men, and not men for the Sabbath, [8] Therefore the Son of Man is also the Lord of the Sabbath." [9] Or have you not read in the Law that on the Sabbath the Priests in the Temple profane the Sabbath, and are blameless? [10] Yet, I say to you that in this place there is One Greater than the Temple. [11] And when you had known what this means, "I desire mercy and not sacrifice (Hosea 6"6) you would not have condemned the guiltless.

3 Healing on the Sabbath

[12] Now it happened on another Sabbath, also, that He entered the Synagogue and Taught. And a man was there, whose right hand was

withered. [13] So the Scribes and Pharisees watched Him closely, whether He would heal on the Sabbath, that they might find and accusation against Him. [14] And He knew their thoughts, and said to the man who had the withered hand, "Arise and stand here." And he arose and stood.

[15] Then Jesus said to them, "I will ask you one thing; is it lawful on the Sabbath to do good or to do evil, to save life or to destroy." [16] And when He had looked around at them all, He said to him, "Stretch out your hand." And he did so, and his hand was restored. [17] Then the Pharisees went out and immediately plotted with the Herodians against Him, how they might destroy Him.

4 Do not judge

[18] "Judge not, and you shall not be judged. Condemn not, and you shall not be condemned. Forgive, and you will be forgiven. [19] Give, and it will be given to you: good measure, pressed down, shaken together, and running over will be put into your bosom.

For with the same measure that you use, it will be measured back to you." [20] And He spoke a parable to them: Can a blind lead the blind? Will they not both fall into a ditch? [21] A disciple is not above his/her teacher, and everyone who is perfectly trained will be like his/her teacher.

[22] And why do you look at the speck in your brother's/sister's eye, and do not perceive the plank in your own eye. [23] Or how can you say to your brother/sister, brother /sister, let me remove the speck that is in your eye; HYPOCRITE! First remove the plank from your own eye, and then you will see clearly to remove the speck that is in your own brother's/sister's eye. [24] "Do not give what is holy to the dogs; nor cast your pearl before swine, lest they tremble them under their feet, and turn and tear you in pieces."

5 Do good to please God

[25] "Take heed that you do not do your charitable deeds before men, to be seen by them. Otherwise, you have no reward from your Father in Heaven. [26] Therefore when you do a charitable deed, do not sound a trumpet before you as the hypocrites do in the Synagogues and in the

streets, that your charitable deed may be in secret; and your Father who sees in secret will Himself reward you."

6 Fasting to be seen only by God

[27] "Moreover, when you fast, do not be like the hypocrites with a sad countenance, for they disfigure their faces that they may appear to men to be fasting. Assuredly, I say to you, they have their reward. [28] And you, when you fast, anoint your head and wash your face, [29] so that you do not appear to men to be fasting, and to your Father's Who sees in secret will reward you."

7 Lay up treasures in Heaven

[30] Do not lay up for yourselves treasures on earth, where moth and rust destroy and thieves break and steal; [31] only, lay up for yourself treasures in Heaven, where neither moth nor rust destroys and thieves do not break in and steal. [32] For where your treasures is' there your heart will be also.

8 The lamp of the body

[33] "No one, when he/she has lit a lamp, puts it in a secret place or under a basket, except one lampstand, that those who come in may see the light. [34] The lamp of the body is the eye. Therefore, when your eye is good, your old body also is full of Light. And your eye is bad, your body also is full of darkness. [35] Therefore take heed that the Light which is in you is not darkness. [36] And supposing then your whole body is full of Light, as when the bright shining of a lamp gives you light." [37] And supposing therefore the light that is in you is darkness, how great is that darkness!

9 You cannot serve God and riches

[38] "No one can serve two masters; for either he/she will hate the one and love the other, or else he/she will be loyal to the one and despises the other. You cannot serve God and mammon."

10 Jesus forgives and heal a paralytic

[39] Now it happened on a certain day, as He was Teaching, that they were Pharisees and teachers of the Law sitting buy, who had come out

of every town of Galilee, Judea, and Jerusalem. And the POWER of the Lord was present with Him to heal. [40] Then Behold, men brought on a bed a man who was paralyzed, whom they sought to bring in and lay before Him. [41] And when they could not find out they might bring him in, because of the crowd, they went up on the house top and let him down with his bed through the tiling into the midst before Jesus. [42] When He saw their faith, He said to him, "man your sins are forgiven you." [43] And the Scribes and the Pharisees began to reason, saying, "Who is this who speaks blasphemies? Who can forgive sins except God alone "?

[44] And when Jesus perceived their thoughts, He answered and said to them, "Why are you reasoning in your heart? [45] Which is easier to say," your sins are forgiven you or to say rise up and walk? [46] "And that you may know that the Son of Man has POWER on earth to forgive sins." He said to the man who was paralyzed. "I say to you, arise, take up your bed and go to your house." [47] Immediately he rose up before them, took up what he had been lying on, and departed to his own house, glorifying God. [48] And they were all amazed, and they glorified God and were filled with fear, saying, "We have seen strange things today!"

11 Jesus pronounces Woe

[49] And woe to you who are rich, for you have received your consolation. [50] Woe to you, who are full, for you shall hunger. Woe to you who laugh now, for you shall mourn and weep. [51] Woe when all men speak well of you, for so did their fathers to the false prophets.

12 I never knew you

[52] "Not everyone who says to Me "LORD "shall enter the Kingdom of Heaven, only, he/she who does the will of My Father in Heaven. [53] Many will say to Me in that day "LORD LORD", have we not prophesied in Your Name, cast out demons in Your Name, and done many wonders in Your Name. [54] And then I will declare to them, "I never knew you" depart from Me, you who practice lawlessness"

CHAPTER 10

1 Woe to the impenitent cities

[1] Then He began to rebuke the cities in which most of His mighty works had been done, because they did not repent [2] Woe, to you Chorazin! "Woe to you Bethsaida! For when the mighty works which were done in you had been done in Tyre and Sidon, they would have repented long ago in sackcloth and ashes. [3] And I say to you, it will be tolerable for Tyre and Sidon in the day of judgment than for you. [4] And you Capharnaum, will you be exalted to Heaven? No, you will be brought down to Hades; and when the mighty works which were done in you had been done in Sidon, it would remain until this day. [5] And I say to you that it shall be more tolerable for the land of Sidon in the day of judgment than for you."

2 Preaching in Galilee

[6] Now in the morning, having risen a long while before daylight, He went out and departed to a solitary place; and there He prayed. [7] And Simon and those who were with him searched for Him. [8] When they found Him, they said to Him, everyone is looking for You." [9] And He said to them, "Let us go into the next towns, that I may preach there also, because for this purpose I have come forth." [10] And He was preaching in their synagogue throughout all Galilee, and casting demons.

3 A house divided cannot stand

[11] And He was casting out a demon, and it was mute. So it was, when the demon had gone out, that the mute spoke; and the multitudes marveled. [12] And some of them (religious leaders) when they heard

about this, try to lay hold of Him, for they said, "He is out of His mind." [13] And the Scribes who came down from Jerusalem said, "He has Beelzebul," and, "By the ruler of the demons He cast out demons."

[14] Others, testing Him, sought a sign from Heaven. [15] And He knowing their thoughts said to them: "Every Kingdom divided again itself is brought to desolation, and a house divided again a house fall. [16] So when Satan also is divided against himself, how will his kingdom stand? Because you say I cast out demons by Beelzebul, [17] and when I cast out demons by Beelzebul, by whom did your sons cast them out? Therefore, they will be your judges. [18] And when I cast out demons with the finger of God, surely the Kingdom of God came upon you.

[19] When a strong man, fully armed, guards his/her own place, his/her goods are in peace. [20] And when a stronger that he/she comes upon him/her and overcomes him/her, he/she takes from him/her all his armor in which he/she trusted, and divides his/her spoils. [21] He/She who is not with Me is against Me, and he/she also does not gather with Me, scatters.

4 Do not worry

[22] Then He said to his Apostles, "Therefore I say to you, do no worry about your life, what you will eat; nor about the body, what you will put on. [23] Life is more than food, and the body is more than clothing. [24] Considers the ravens, for they neither sow nor reap, which have neither storehouse nor barn; and God feed them. Of how much more value are you than the birds. [25] And which of you by worrying can add one cubit to his /her stature? [26] And you then are not able to do the least, why are you anxious for the rest? [27] Considers the lilies, how they grow: they neither tail or spin; and yet I say to you, even Solomon in all his glory was not arranged like one of these. [28] And when then God so clothed the grass, which today is in the field and tomorrow is thrown into the oven, how much more will He clothed you, O you of little faith?

[29] "And do not seek what you should eat or what you should drink, nor have an anxious mind. [30] For all these things the nations of the world seek after, and your Father knows that you need these things. [31] Only seek the Kingdom of God, and these things should be added to you.

[32] Do not fear, "little flock" (everyone), for it is your Father's good pleasure to give you the Kingdom. [33] Sell what you have and give alms; provide yourselves money bags which do not grow old, a treasure in the Heavens that does not fail, where no thieve approaches nor moth destroys. [34] For where your treasure is, there your heart will be also. [35] Therefore do not worry about tomorrow, for tomorrow will worry about its own things, sufficient for the day is its own trouble.

5 Keep asking, seeking, knocking

[36] "Ask, and it will be given to you; seek and you will find; knock, and it will be opened to you. [37] For everyone who ask receives, and also who seeks find, and to him/her who knocks it will be opened. [38] Or what man/woman among you how, when his/her son/ daughter asks for bread will give him/her a stone? [39] Or when he/she asked for a fish will he/she give him/her a serpent? Or asking for and egg, will he/she give him/her a scorpion? [40] When you then, being evil know how to give good gifts to your children, how much more will your Father Who is in Heaven give good things to those who ask Him. [41] Therefore, whatever you want men/women to do to you, do also to them, for this is the Law and the Prophets. [42] How much more will your Heavenly Father give the Holy Spirit to those who ask Him.

6 The narrow way

[43] And He went through the cities and villages, Teaching, and journeying toward Jerusalem. [44] Then one said to Him, "Lord, are there few who are saved? "And He said to them, [45] "Enter by the narrow gate; for wide is the gate and broad is the way that leads to destruction, and there is many who go in by it. [46] How narrow is the gate and difficult is the way which leads to life, and there are few who find it. [47] Strive to enter through the narrow gate, for many I say to you, will seek to enter and will not be able."

[48] When once the Master of the house has risen up and shut the door, and you begin to stand outside and knock at the door, saying, "Lord, Lord opens for us", and He will answer and say to you, I do not know you, where are you from? [49] Then you will begin to say, we ate and drank in Your presence, and you Taught in our streets. [50] And He

will say, I tell you I do not know you, where are you from? Depart from Me, all you workers of iniquity.

[51] There will be weeping and gnashing of the teeth, when you'll see Abraham Isaac and Jacob and all the Prophets in the Kingdom of God, and yourselves thrust out. [52] They will come from the east and the west, from the north and the south, and sit down in the Kingdom of God. [53] "And indeed there are last who will be first, and there are first who will be last."

[54] In that very day some Pharisees came, saying to Him, "Get out and depart from here, for Herod wants to kill You." [55] And He said to them, "Go tell that fox, Behold, I cast out demons and perform cures today and tomorrow, and the fourth day shall I be perfected! [56] Nevertheless I must journey today, tomorrow, and the day following; for it cannot be that a Prophet should perish outside of Jerusalem."

CHAPTER 11

1 You will know them by their fruits

[1] "Beware of false prophets, who come to you in sheep's clothing, and inwardly they are ravenous wolves." [2] For every tree is known by its own fruit. For men do not gather figs from thorns, nor do they gather grapes from a bramble bush. [3] Even so, every good tree bears good fruit, and a bad tree bears bad fruit. [4] A good tree cannot bear bad fruit, nor can a bad tree bear good fruit.

[5] Every tree that does not bear good fruit is cut down and thrown into the fire. [6] Therefore by their fruits you will know them. [7] A good man/woman out of the good treasure of his/her heart bring forth good; and an evil man/woman out of the evil treasure of his/her heart bring forth evil. For out of the abundance of his/her heart his/her mouth speaks.

2 Jesus healed a centurion servant

[8] Now when Jesus entered Capharnaum, a centurion came to him, pleading Him, saying, [9] "Lord, my servant is lying at home paralyzed, dreadfully tormented." [10] And Jesus said to him, "I will come and heal him." [11] The centurion answered to Him "Lord", I am not worthy that You should come under my roof. Except, only speak a word, and my servant will be healed. [12] For I also am a man under authority, having soldiers under me. And I say to the one, "Go" and he goes; and to another, "Come", and he comes; and to my servant, "Do this" and he does it."

[13] When Jesus heard it, He marveled, and said to those who followed, "Assuredly, I say to you, I have not found such great faith, not even in Israel! [14] And I say to you that many will come from east and

west, and sit down with Abraham, Isaac, and Jacob in The Kingdom of Heaven.

¹⁵ And the sons/daughters of Satan's kingdom will be cast out into other darkness. There will be weeping and gnashing of teeth." ¹⁶ Then Jesus said to the centurion, "Go your way, and as you have believed, so let it be done to you." And his servant was healed that same hour.

3 Many healed in evening

¹⁷ When evening had come, they brought to Him many who were demon-possessed. And He cast out the spirits with a word, and healed all who were sick, ¹⁸ that it might be fulfilled which was spoken by Isaiah the Prophet, saying:

He Himself took our infirmities and bore our sicknesses. (Isaiah 53:4)

4 The cost of discipleship

¹⁹ And when Jesus saw great multitudes about Him, He gave a command to depart to the other side. ²⁰ Then a certain Scribe came and said to Him, "Teacher, I will follow You wherever You go." ²¹ And Jesus said to him, "Foxes have holes and birds of the air has nests, and the Son of Man has no where to lay His head."

²² Then another of His Disciples said to Him, "Lord let me first go and bury my father." ²³ And Jesus said to him, "Follow Me, and let the dead bury their own dead, and you go and preach the Kingdom of God." ²⁴ And another also said, "Lord, I will follow You, only let me first go and bid them farewell who are at my house." ²⁵ And Jesus said to him, "No one, having put his hand to the plow, and looking back, is fit for the Kingdom of God."

5 A great multitude follow Jesus

²⁶ And Jesus withdrew with His Apostles to the sea. And a great multitude from Galilee followed Him, and from Judea and Jerusalem and Idumea and beyond the Jordan; and those from Tyre and Sidon, a great multitude, when they heard how many things He was doing, came to Him. ²⁷ So He told His Disciples that a small boat should be

kept ready for Him because of the multitude, lest they should crush Him.

²⁸ For He healed many, so that as many who had afflictions pressed about Him to touch Him. ²⁹ And the unclean spirits, whenever they saw Him, fell down before Him and cried out and saying, "You are the Son of God." ³⁰ And He sternly warned them that they should not make Him known.

<u>6 A demon-possessed man healed</u>

³¹ Then they sailed to the country of the Gadarenes, which is opposite Galilee. ³² And when He stepped out on the land, there He met a certain man from the city who had demons for a long time. And he wore no clothes, nor did he live in a house only in the tombs. ³³ When he saw Jesus, he cried out, fell down before Him, and with a loud voice said, "What have I to do with You, Jesus, Son of the Most High God? I beg You, do not torment me!"

³⁴ For He had commanded the unclean spirit to come out of the man. For it had often seized him, and he was kept under guard, bound with chains and shackles: and he broke the bonds and was driven by the demons into the wilderness. ³⁵ Jesus asked him, saying, "What is your name?" And he said, "Legion", because many demons had entered him. ³⁶ And they begged Him that He would not command them to go into the ABYSS.

³⁷ Nom a herd of many swine was feeding there on the mountain. And they begged Him that He would permit them to enter them. And He permitted them. ³⁸ Then the demons went out of the man and entered the swine, and the herd ran violently down the steep place into the lake and drowned. ³⁹ When those who feed them saw what had happened, they fled and told it in the city and in the country. ⁴⁰ Then they went out to see what had happened, and came to Jesus, and found the man from whom the demons had departed, sitting at the feet of Jesus, clothed and in his right mind.

And they were afraid. ⁴¹ They also who had seen it, and told them by what means he who had been demon- posses was healed. ⁴² Then the whole multitude of the surrounding region of the Gadarenes ask Him to depart from them, for they were seized with great fear. And He got into the boat and returned. [43] Now the man from whom the demons had departed begged Him that he might be with Him. And Jesus sent him away, saying, "Return to your own house, and tell what great things God had done for you." And he went his way and proclaimed through out the whole city what great things Jesus had done for him.

CHAPTER 12

1 The unpardonable sin

[1] "Therefore I say to you, every sin and blasphemy will be forgiven men and the blasphemy against the Spirit will not be forgiven men. [2] Anyone who speaks a word against the Son of Man, it will be forgiven him/her; and whoever speaks against the Holy Spirit, it will not be forgiven him/her, either in this age or in the age to come."

2 Build on rock

[3] And why do you call Me "Lord, Lord", and do not do the things that I say? [4] Whoever comes to Me, and hears My saying and does them, I will show you who he/she is like: [5] He/She is like a man/woman building a house, who dug deep and laid the foundation on the rock. And when the flood arose, the stream beat vehemently against the house, and could not shake it, for it was founded on the rock.

[6] And he/she who heard and did nothing is like a man/woman who build a house on the earth without the foundation, against which the stream beat vehemently; and immediately collapsed. And the ruin of that house was great. [7] And so it was, when Jesus had ended these saying, that the people were astonished at His Teaching, [8] for He Taught them as One having Authority, and not as a Scribes.

3 Jesus, mother and brothers send for Him

[9] While He was still talking to the multitudes, Behold, His mother and His brothers stood outside, seeking to talk to Him. [10] Then one said to Him, "Look Your mother and Your brothers are standing outside, to speak to You." And He answered and said to the one who told Him, [11] "who is My mother and who are My brothers and sisters." [12] And He

stretched out His hand toward His Apostles and said, "Here are My mother and My brothers and My sisters! [13] For who ever does the will of My Father in Heaven is My brother, My sister and My mother."

4 A girl restored to life and a woman healed

[14] Now when Jesus had crossed over again by boat to the other side, a great multitude gathered to Him; and He was by the sea. [15] And Behold, one of the rulers of the Synagogue come, Jairus by name. And when he saw Him, he fell at His feet [16] and begged Him earnestly saying, "My little daughter lies at the point of death. Come and lay Your hands on her, that she may be healed, and she will live." [17] So Jesus went with him, and a great multitude followed Him and thronged Him.

[18] Now a certain woman had a flow of blood for twelve years, [19] and had suffered many things from many physicians. She had spent all that she had and was not better, only rather grew worse. [20] When she heard about Jesus, she came behind Him in the crowd and touches His garment. [21] For she said, "Only I may touch His clothes, I shall be made well." [22] Immediately the fountain of her blood was dried up, and she felt in her body that she was healed of the affliction. [23] And Jesus, immediately knowing in Himself that POWER had gone out of Him, turned around in the crowd and said, "Who touched My clothes?" [24] And His Disciples said to Him, "You see the multitude thronging You, and You said "Who touched Me?" (Jesus never said who touched Me, He said who touched my clothes. So, we as humans we don't always repeat what we did heard in the first place, well, -- most likely we do, ------ and most likely, --- well--- we don't.

[25] And He looked around to see her who had done this thing. [26] And the woman, fearing and trembling, knowing what had happened to her, came and fell down before Him and told Him the whole truth. [27] And He said to her, "Daughter, your faith has made you well. Go in peace, and be healed of the affliction."

[28] While He was still speaking, some came from the ruler of the Synagogue's house and said, "Your daughter is dead. Why trouble the Teacher any further?" [29] As soon as Jesus heard the word that was spoken, He said to the ruler of the Synagogue, "Do not be afraid; only

believe." ³⁰ And He permitted no one to follow Him except Peter, James, and John the brother of James. ³¹ Then He came to the house of the ruler of the Synagogue, and saw a tumult and those who wept and wailed loudly.

³² When He came in, He said to them, "Why make the commotion and weep? The child is not dead, only sleeping." ³³ And they ridiculed Him. And when He had put them all outside, He took the father and the mother of the child, and those who were with Him, and entered where the child was lying. ³⁴ Then He took the child by the hand, and said to her, Talitha cumin which is translated "Little girl, I say to you arise." ³⁵ Immediately the girl arose and walked, for she was twelve years of age. And they were overcome with great amazement. ³⁶ And He commanded them strictly that no one should know it, and said that something should be given to her to eat.

5 Wind and wave obey Jesus

³⁷ Now it happened on a certain day, that He got into a boat with His Apostles. And He said to them, "Let us cross over the other side of the lake." And they launched out. ³⁸ And as they sail, He fell asleep. And a windstorm came down on the lake, and they came to Him and awoke Him, saying, "Master, Master, we are perishing?" Then He arose and rebuked the wind and said to the sea "Peace, be still." ³⁹ And He said to them, "Why are you so fearful? Why is it that you have no faith?" And they were afraid and marveled at the same time. (WHAT A BUNCH!!!!!!!!) And they were wondering, how can this be.

For He commanded even the winds and water, and they obey Him!

6 John the Baptist exalt Christ

⁴⁰ After these things Jesus and His Disciples came into the land of Judea, and there He remained with them and Baptizing peoples. ⁴¹ Now John (the Baptist) also was Baptizing in Aenon near Salim, because there was much water there. And they came and were Baptized. ⁴² For John had not been put in prison (yet). ⁴³ Then there arose a dispute between some of John's disciples and the Jews about purification.

⁴⁴ And they came to John and said to him, "Rabbi", He Who was with you beyond the Jordan, to Whom you have testified—Behold, He

is Baptizing, and all are coming to Him." [45] John answered and said, "a man/woman can receive nothing unless it has been given to him/her from Heaven. [46] You yourselves bear me witness, that I said, "I am not the Christ, and, I have been sent before Him." [47] He who has the Bride is the Bridegroom; and the friend of the Bridegroom, who stands and hears Him, rejoices greatly because of the Bridegroom voice. Therefore, this joy of mine is fulfilled.

[48] He must increase, and I must decrease. [49] He Who comes from above is above all, he/she who is of the earth is earthly and speaks of the earth, He Who come from Heaven is above all. [50] And what He has seen and heard, that He testifies; and no one receives His testimony. [51] He who has received His testimony has certified that God is True. [52] For He Whom God has sent speaks the Words of God, For God does not give the Spirit, by measure. [53] The Father loves the Son, and has given all things into His hands. [54] He/She who believes in the Son has Everlasting Life; and he/she who does not believe the Son shall not see life, and the wrath of God abides on him/her."

CHAPTER 13

1 Two blinded men healed

¹ When Jesus departed from there, two blinded men followed Him, crying out and saying, "Son of David, have mercy on us?!" ² And when He had come into the house, the blind men came to Him. And Jesus said to them, "Do you believe that I Am able to do this?" They say to Him, "Yes, Lord." ³ Then He touched their eyes, saying, "According to your faith let it be to you." ⁴ And their eyes were opened. And Jesus sternly warned them, saying "See that no one knows it." ⁵ And when they had departed, they spread the news about Him in all that country.

2 A mute man speaks

⁶ As they went out, Behold, they brought to Him a man mute and demon-possessed. ⁷ And when the demon was cast out, the mute spoke. And the multitudes marveled, saying, "it was never seen like this in Israel." ⁸ And the Pharisees said, "He cast out demons by the ruler of the demons."

3 The compassion of Jesus

⁹ Then Jesus went about all the cities and villages, Teaching in their Synagogue, Preaching the Gospel of the Kingdom, and healing every sickness and every disease. ¹⁰ And when He saw the multitudes, He was moved with compassion for them, because they were harassed and scattered, like sheep having no Shepherd. ¹¹ Then He said to His Apostles, "The harvest truly is plentiful, and the laborers are few. ¹² Therefore pray the Lord of the harvest to send out laborers into His harvest."

4 Sending out the twelve

[13] These twelve Jesus sent out and commanded them, saying, "Do not go into the way of the Gentiles, and do not enter a city of the Samaritans. Only go rather to the lost sheep of the house of Israel. [14] Then He called His twelve Apostles together and gave them Power and Authority over all demons, and to cure diseases. [15] And as you go, preach, saying, the Kingdom of Heaven is at hand." [16] Heal the sick, cleanse the lepers, raise the dead, cast out demons. Freely you have received, freely give.

[17] He commanded to take nothing for the journey except a staff— no bag, no bread, no copper in their money belts— [18] and to wear sandals, and not to put on two tunics. [19] Also He said to them," In whatever place you enter a house, stay there till you depart from the place. [20] And whoever will not receive you, when you go out of the city, shake off the very dust from your feet as a testimony against them. [21] So they went out and preach that people should repent. [22] And they cast out many demons, and anointed with oil many who were sick, and healed them.

5 Persecutions are coming

[23] "Behold, I send you out as a sheep in the midst of wolves." Therefore, be wise as serpents and harmless as a dove. [24] And beware of men, for they will delivers you up to the councils and scourge you in the Synagogues. [25] You will be brought before Governors and Kings for My sake, as a testimony to them and to the Gentiles. [26] And when they deliver you up, do not worry about how or what you should speaks. [27] For it is not you who speaks, it is the Spirit of your Father who speak in you.

[28] Now brother will deliver up brother to death, and a father his child; and children will raise up against parents and cause them to be put to death. [29] And you will be hated by all for My Name's sake, and he/she who endures to the end will be saved. [30] When they persecute you in this city, flee to another. For assuredly, I say to you, you will not have gone through the cities of Israel before the Son of Man comes.

[31] A disciple is not above his/her teacher, nor a servant above his/her master. [32] It is enough for a disciple that he/she be like his/her

teacher, and a servant like the master. Supposing they have called the master of the house Beelzebul, how much more will they call those of his/her household! [33] Therefore do not fear them. For there is nothing covered that will not be revealed, and hidden that will not be known.

6 Jesus Teaches the fear of the Lord

[34] Whatever I tell you in the dark, speak in the light; and what you hear in the ear, preach on the housetops. [35] And do not fear those who kill the body and do not kill the soul. And rather fear Him who is able to destroy both soul and body in hell. [36] Are not two sparrows sold for a copper coin? [37] And the very hairs of your head are all numbered. [38] Do not fear therefore; you are of more value than many sparrows.

CHAPTER 14

1 Confess, Christ before men

¹ Therefore whoever confesses Me before men, him/her I will also deny you before My Father Who is in Heaven. ² And whoever denies Me before men, him/her I will also deny you before My Father Who is in Heaven.

2 Christ bring division

³ Do not think that I came to bring peace on earth. I did not come to bring peace except a sword. ⁴ For I have come to set a man/woman against his/her father, a daughter/son against her/his mother, and a daughter-in-law/son-in-law against her/his mother-in-law/father-law; ⁵ he/she who loves father or mother more than Me is not worthy of Me. ⁶ and he/she who does not take his/her cross and follow after Me is not worthy of Me. ⁷ He/She who find his/her life will lose it, and he/she who loves his/her life for My sake will find it.

3 A cup of cold water

⁸ He/she who receives you receives Me, and he/she who receives Me receives Him Who sent Me. ⁹ He/She who receives a Prophet in the name of a Prophet shall receive a Prophet's reward. And he/she who receives a righteous man/woman in the name of a righteous shall receive a righteous man's/woman's reward. ¹⁰ And whoever gives one of these little one only a cup of cold water in the name of a disciple, assuredly, I say to you, he/she shall by no means lose his/her reward.

4 John the Baptist sends messengers to Jesus

¹¹ Now it came to pass, when Jesus finished commanding His twelve Apostles, that He departed from there to Teach and to Preach

in their cities. [12] And when john had heard in prison about the works of, Christ, he sent two of his disciples [13] and said to Him, "are You the, coming One, or do we look for another?" [14] Jesus answered and said to them, go and tell John the things which you hear and see: [15] The blind, sees and the lame walk; the lepers are cleanse and the deaf hear; the dead are raised up and the poor have the Gospel preached to them. [16] And blessed is he/she who is not offended because of Me.

[17] As they departed, Jesus began to say to the multitudes concerning John: "What did you go out into the wilderness to see? A reed shaken by the wind? [18] And what did you go out to see? A man clothed in soft garments indeed, those who were soft clothing are in King's houses. [19] And what did you go out to see? A Prophet? Yes. I say to you, and more than a Prophet. [20] For this is he of whom it is written: "Behold, I send a messenger before Your face, who will prepare Your way before You:"

"Assuredly, I say to you, among those born of woman there has not risen one greater than John the Baptist; and he/she who is least in the Kingdom of Heaven is greater than he. [22] And from the days of John the Baptist until now the Kingdom of Heaven suffers violence, and the violent take it by force. [23] For all the Prophets and the Law prophesied until John. [24] And you are willing to receive it, he is Elijah who is to come. [25] He/She who has ears to hear, let him/her hear.

[26] And to what shall I liken this generation? It is liken children sitting in the marketplaces and calling to their companions, and saying: "We play the flute for you, and you did not dance; we mourn to you; and you did not lament." [27] For john came neither eating nor drinking, and they say, "He has a demon." [28] The Son of Man came eating and drinking, and they say, "look a glutton and a winebibber, a friend of tax collectors and sinners!" And Wisdom is justified by Her works.

5 Jesus gives True rest

[29] At that time Jesus answered and said, "I Thank You, Father, Lord of Heaven and Earth, that You have hidden these things from the wise and prudent and have revealed them to babes. [30] Even so, Father, for it seemed good in Your sight. [31] All things have been delivered to Me by My Father, and no one knows the Son except the Father. Nor does anyone know the Father except the Son, and the one to whom The Son

wills to reveal Him. [32] Come to Me, all you who labor and are heavy laden, and I will give you rest.

[33] Take My yoke upon you and learn from Me, for I am gentle and lowly in heart, and you find rest for your soul. [34] My yoke is easy and My burden is light."

6 Behold, My Servant

[35] And when Jesus knew it, He withdrew from there. And great multitudes followed Him, and He healed them all. [36] Yet He warned them not to make Him known, [37] that He might be fulfilled which was spoken by Isaiah the Prophet saying: [38] "Behold! My servant Whom I have chosen, My beloved in Whom My soul is well please! I will put My Spirit upon Him, and He will declare justice to the Gentiles.

[39] He will not quarrel nor cry out, nor anyone hear His voice in the streets. A bruised reed He will not break, and smoking flax He will not quench, till He sends forth justice to victory; and in His Name Gentiles will trust."

CHAPTER 15

1 The Scribes and Pharisees ask for a sign

¹ Then some of the Scribes and Pharisees answered saying, "Teacher we want to see a sign from You." ² And He answered and said to them, "And evil and adulterous generation seeks after a sign, and no will be given to it except the sign of the Prophet Jonah. ³ For as Jonah was three days and three nights in the belly of the great fish, so will the Son of Man be three days and three nights in the heart of the earth. **I TOLD PEOPLE FOR YEARS, THAT JESUS DID ACTUALLY RESURRECTED ON THE FOURTH DAY, NOT ON THE THIRD DAY AS 99.9 % AS PEOPLE SAY, AND EVEN THE PEOPLE IN THE BIBLE ARE INCORRECT. I SPEAK TO MANY PREACHERS AND THEY ALL DISMISS ME LIKE THE RELIGIOUS JEWS DISMISSED JESUS AS THEIR SAVIOR AND KING. TRY TO REMEMBERING YOUR MATH. THAT 3 DAYS AND 3 NIGHTS, = 72 HOURS, --- "NOW AFTER THE SABBATH, AS THE FIRST DAY OF THE WEEK BEGAN TO DAWN." The first day of the week is always Sunday. (In the time of Jesus and in our present time) HOPEFULLY YOU WILL STOP SAYING THAT JESUS RESURRECTED ON THE THIRD DAY. ----Right.**

⁴ The men of Nineveh will rise up in the judgment with this generation and condemn it, because they repented at the preaching of Jonah; and indeed, a greater than Jonah is here. ⁵ The Queen of the south will rise up in the judgment with this generation and condemn it, for she came from the ends of the earth to hear the Wisdom of Solomon; and indeed, a greater than Solomon is here.

2 An unclean spirit returns

[6] "When an unclean spirit goes out of a man/woman, he goes through dry places, seeking rest, and find none. [7] Then he say's, "I will return to my house from which I came." And when he comes, he finds it empty swept, and put in order. [8] Then he goes and takes with him seven others spirit's more wicked than himself, and they enter and dwell there; and the last state of that man/woman is worst than the first. So shall it also be with this wicked generation."

3 The parable of the Sower

[9] On the same day Jesus went out of the house and sat by the sea. [10] And a great multitude were gathered together to Him, so that He got into a boat and sat; and the whole multitude stood on the shore. [11] Then He spoke many things to them in parables, saying: "Behold, a Sower's went out to sow. [12] And as He sowed, some seed fell by the wayside; and the birds came and devoured them. [13] Some fell in stony places, where they did not have much earth; and they immediately sprang up because they had no depth of earth.

[14] And when the sun was up, they were scorched, and because they had no root they withered away. [15] And some fell among thorns, and the thorns sprang up and choke them. [16] And others fell on Good Ground and yielded a crop: some a hundredfold some sixty, some thirty. [17] He/She who has ears to hear let him/her hear!"

4 The purpose of parables

[18] And the Disciples came and said to Him, "Why do You speak to them in parables?" [19] He answered and said to them, "Because it has been given to you to know the mysteries of the Kingdom of Heaven, and to them it has not been given. [20] For whoever has to him/her, more will be Given, and he/she will have abundance; and whoever does have, even what he/she had will be taken away from him/her. [21] Therefore I speak to them in parables, because seeing they do not see, and hearing they do not hear, nor do they understand. [22] And in the Prophecy of Isaiah (Isaiah 6:9) it said, [23] "They keep on hearing and do not understand; they keep on seeing and do not perceive. [24] And Blessed are your eyes for they see, and your ears for they hear; [25] for

assuredly, I say to you that many Prophets and righteous men desired to see what you see, and did not see it, and to hear what you hear, and did not hear it."

5 The parable of the Sower explained

[26] And He said to them, "Do you understand this parable? How then will you understand all parables? [27] The Sower sows the Word. [28] And these are the one by the wayside where the Word of God is sown. When they hear, Satan comes immediately and takes away the Word that was sown in their hearts. [29] These likewise are the ones sown on stony ground who, when they hear the Word, immediately receive it with gladness; [30] and they have no root in themselves, and so endure only for a time. Afterward, when tribulation or persecution, arises from the Word's sake, immediately stumble.

[31] And these are the ones sown among thorns; they are the ones who hear the Word, [32] and the cares of this world, the deceitfulness of riches, and the desire of other things entering in choke the Word, and it become unfruitful. [33] And these are the ones sown on good ground, those who hear the Word, accept it, and bear fruit: some thirtyfold, some sixty, and some hundred."

6 The model prayer

[34] And when you pray, you shall not be like the hypocrites. For they love to pray standing in the Synagogues and on the corners of the streets, that they may be seen by men. Assuredly, I say to you, they have their reward. [35] And you, when you pray, go into your room, and when you shut your door, pray to your Father who is in the secret place; and your Father who sees in secret will reward you.

[36] And when you pray, do not use vain repetitions as the heathen do. For they think that they will be heard for their many words. [37] Therefore do not be like them. For the Father know the things you have need of before you ask Him. [38] In this manner, therefore pray: Our Father in Heaven, allowed be Your Name. [39] Your Kingdom come. Your will be done on earth as it is in Heaven.

[40] Give us this day our daily Bread. [41] And forgive our sins, as we forgive others. [42] And give us the strength to not fall into temptation,

For Yours is the Kingdom and the Power and the glory forever. Amen. [43] For when you forgive men their trespasses, Your Heavenly Father will also forgive you. [44] And when you do not forgive men their trespasses, neither will your Father's forgive your trespasses.

CHAPTER 16

1 The parable of the wheat and the tares

[1] Another parable He put forth to them, saying, "The Kingdom of Heaven is like a man /woman who sowed good seed in his/her field; [2] and when he/she men slept, his/her enemy came and sowed tares among the wheat and went his/her way. [3] And when the grain had sprouted and produces a crop, then the tares also appeared. [4] So the servants of the owner come and said to him/her, "Did you not sow good seed in your field? How then does it have tares?" [5] He/She said to them, "An enemy has done this." The servants said to him/her "Do you want us then to go and gather them up?" [6] And he/she said, "No, lest while you gather up the tares you also uproot the wheat with them."

[7] Let both grow together until the harvest, and at the time of harvest I will say to the reapers,' first gather together the tares and bind them in bundles to burn them, and gather the wheat into your barn."

2 The parable of the mustard seed

[8] Then He said, "To what shall we liken the Kingdom of God? Or with what parable shall we picture it. [9] It is like a mustard seed which, when it is sown on the ground, is smaller than all seeds on earth; [10] and when it is sown, it grows up and becomes greater than all herbs, and shoots out large branches, so that the birds of the air may nest under its shade."

3 The parable of the leaven

[11] Another parable He spoke to them: "The Kingdom of Heaven is like leaven, which a woman/man took and hid in three measures of meal till it was all leavened."

4 Prophecy and the parable

[12] All these things Jesus spoke to the multitude in parables; and without a parable He did not speak to them, [13] that it might be fulfilled which was spoken by the Prophet, saying, "I will open My mouth in parables; I will utter things kept secret from the foundation of the world." (Ps: 78:2)

5 The parable of the tares explained

[14] Then Jesus sent the multitude away and went into the house. And His Apostles come to Him, saying, "Explain to us the parable of the tares of the field." [15] He answered and said to them: "He/She who sows the good seed is the Son of Man. [16] The field is the world, the good seed is the sons/daughter of the Kingdom, and the tares are the sons /daughters of the wicked one. [17] The enemy who sowed them is the devil, the harvest is the end of the age, and the reapers are the Angels. [18] Therefore as the tares are gathered and burn in the fire, so it will be at the end of this age. [19] The Son of Man will send out His Angels, and they will gather out of His Kingdom all things that offend, and those who practice lawlessness, [20] and will cast them into the furnace of fire.

There will be wailing and gnashing of teeth. [21] Then the righteous will shine forth as the sun in the Kingdom of their Father. He/She who also has ears to hear, let him/her hear!

6 The parable of the hidden treasure

[22] Again, the Kingdom of Heaven is like treasure hidden in the field, which a man /woman found and hid; and joy over it he/she goes and sells all that he/she had and buys the field.

7 The parable of the pearl of great price

[23] Again, the Kingdom of Heaven is like a merchant seeking beautiful pearls, [24] when he/she had found one pearl of great price, went and sold all that he/she had and bought it.

8 The parable of the dragnet

[25] Again, the Kingdom of Heaven is like a dragnet that was cast into the sea and gathered some of every kind, [26] which, when it was

full, they drew to shore; and they sat down and gathered the good in vessels, and threw the bad away. [27] So it will be at the end of the age. The Angels will come forth, separate the wicked from among the just, [28] and cast them in the furnace of fire. There will be wailing and gnashing of teeth. [29] Have you understand all these things? They said to Him, "Yes Lord."

[30] Then He said to them, "Therefore every Scribe instructed concerning The Kingdom of Heaven is like a householder who brings out of his/her treasure things new and old."

9 John the Baptist beheaded

[31] For Herod himself had sent and laid hold of John, and bound him in prison for the sake of Herodias, his brother Philip's wife; for he had married her. [32] Because John had said to Herod, "It is not lawful for you to have your brother's wife." [33] Therefore he held it against him and wanted to kill him, and she could not; for Herod fear John, knowing that he was a just and holy man, and he protected him. And when he heard him, he did many things, and heard him gladly.

[34] Then an opportune day come when Herod on his birthday gave a feast for his nobles, the high officers, and the chief men of Galilee. [35] And when Herodias's daughter herself came in and danced, and pleased Herod and those who sat with him, the King said to the girl, "Ask me whatever you want, and I will give it to you." [36] He also swear to her, "Whatever you ask me, I will give you, up to half of my kingdom."

[37] So she went out and said to her mother, "What should I ask." And she said, "The head of John the Baptist." [38] Immediately she came in with haste to the King and asked, saying, "I want you to give me at once the head of John the Baptist on the platter." [39] The King was exceedingly sorry; yet, because of the oats and because of those who sat with him, he did not want to refuse her.

[40] Immediately the King sent an executioner and commanded his head to be brought. And he went and beheaded him in prison, [41] brought his head on a platter, and gave it to the girl; and the girl gave it to her mother. [42] When his disciples heard of it, they came and took away his corpse and laid it in a tomb. ------(And after some time)

[43] Now King Herod at that time heard of Jesus, for His name had become well known. And he said, "John the Baptist is risen from the dead, and therefore these POWER are at work in Him." (Jesus) [44] Others said, "It is Elijah." And the others said, "It is the Prophet," This is John, whom I beheaded; he has been raised from the dead.

10 Feeding the five thousand

[46] And the Apostles, when they had returned, they told Him all that they had done and what they had thought. [47] And He said to them, "Come aside by yourselves to a deserted place in the boat by themselves, to a city called Bethsaida (Bethany)." [48] And when the multitudes knew it, they followed Him; and He received them and had compassion for them, because they were like sheep not having a Shepherd. And He began to Teach them many things. [49] When the day was now far spent, His Disciples came to Him and said," This is a deserted place, and already the hour is late

[50] Send them away, that they may go into the surrounding country and villages and buy themselves something to eat." [51] And He answered and said to them, "You give them something to eat? [52] And He said to them, "How many loaves do you have? Go and see", and when they found out they said, "Five loaves and two fish." [53] Then He commanded them to make them all sit down in groups on the green grass.

[54] So they sat down in ranks, in hundreds and fifties. [55] And when He had taken the five loaves and the two fish, He looked up the Heavens, Blessed and break the loaves, and gave them to His Disciples to set before them; and the two fish He divided among them all. [56] And they all ate and were filled. [57] And they took up twelve baskets full of fragments and of the fish. [58] Now those who had eat the loaves were five thousand men besides women and children. [59] Then those men, when they had seen the sign that Jesus did, said, "This is truly the Prophet Who is to come into the world."

11 Jesus walks on the sea

[60] Immediately Jesus made His Apostles get into the boat and go before Him to the other side, while He sent the multitudes away. [61] He went up on the mountain by Himself to pray. Now when evening

came, He was alone there. [62] And the boat was now in many furlongs away from the land, tossed by the waves, for the wind was contrary. [63] Now in the fourth watch of the night Jesus went to them, walking on the sea. [64] And when the Apostles saw Him walking on the sea, they were troubled, saying, "It is a ghost!" And they cried of fear.

[65] And immediately Jesus spoke to them, saying, "Be of good cheer! It is I; do not be afraid." And Peter answered Him and said, "Lord, can You command me to come to You on the water." [66] So he said, "Come" and, Peter had come down out of the boat, he walked on the water to go to Jesus. [67] And when he saw that the wind was boisterous, he was afraid; and immediately Jesus stretched out His hand and caught him, and said to him "O you of little faith why did you doubt?"

[69] And when they got into the boat, the wind ceased. [70] Then those who were in the boat worshiped Him, saying "Truly You are the Son of God."

12 Many touches Him and are made well

[71] When they had crossed over, they came to the land of Gennesaret and anchored there. [72] And when they came out of the boat, immediately the people recognized Him, [73] and ran through surrounding region, and began to carry about on beds those who were sick to wherever they heard He was. [74] Wherever He entered, into villages, cities or the country, they laid the sick in the marketplaces, and begged Him that they might just touch the hem of His garment. And as many as touched Him were made well.

CHAPTER 17

1 Defilement comes from within

[1] Then the Scribes and Pharisees who were from Jerusalem came to Jesus, saying, [2] "Why do Your Disciples transgress the tradition of the elders? For they do not wash their hands when they eat bread." [3] He answered and said to them, "Why do you also transgress the commandment of God because of your tradition? [4] For God commanded, saying, Honor your father and your mother, and, he/she curses father or mother, let him/her be put to death. And you say, whoever says to his father or mother, Whatever profit you might have received from me is a gift to God, [6] Then he/she need not honor his father, thus you have made the word of no effect by your tradition. [7] Hypocrites! Well did Isaiah Prophesy about you, [8] saying, These people draw near to Me with their mouth, and honor Me with their lips, only, their heart is far from Me. [9] And in vain they worship Me, teaching as doctrines the commandments of men."

[10] When He had called the multitude to Himself, He said to them, "Hear and understand: [11] It is not what goes into the mouth that defiles a man/woman; and what comes out of the mouth, defiles a man/woman." [12] Then His Disciples came out and said to Him, "Do You know that the Pharisees were offended when they heard this saying?" [13] And He answered and said, "Every plant that My Heavenly Father has not planted will be up rooted. [14] Let them alone. They are blind leaders of the blind, and when the blind leads the blind, both will fall into a ditch."

[15] Then Peter's answered and said to Him, "Explain this parable to us." [16] And Jesus said are you also still without understanding? [17] Do you not yet understand that whatever enters the mouth goes into the

stomach and is eliminated? And those things which proceeded out of the mouth come from the heart, and they defile a man/woman.

2 A Gentile shows her faith

21 From there He arose and went into the region of Tyre and Sidon, And He entered a house and wanted no one to know it, and He cannot be hidden, 22 For a woman whose young daughter had an unclean spirit heard about Him, and she came and fell at His feet. 23 The woman was a Greek, a Syros-Phoenicians by birth, and she kept asking Him to cast the demon out of her daughter. 24 And Jesus said to her, "Let the children be filled first, for it is not good to take the children's bread and throw it to the little dog."

25 And she answered and said to Him, "Yes, Lord, yet even the little dogs under the table eat from the children crumb's." 26 Then He said to her, "For this saying go your way the demon has gone out of your daughter." 27 And when she had come to the house, she found the demon gone out, and her daughter lying on the bed.

3 Jesus heals a great multitude again

28 Jesus departed from there skirted the sea od Galilee, and went up on the mountain and sat down there. 29 Then great multitudes came to Him, having with them the lame, blind mute, maimed and many others; and they laid them down at Jesus feet, and He heal them. 30 And the multitude marveled when they saw the mute speaking, the maimed made whole, the lame walking, and the blind seeing; and they glorified the God of Israel.

4 Feeding the four thousand

31 Now Jesus called His Apostles to Himself and said, "I have compassion on the multitude, because they have now continued with Me three days and have nothing to eat. And I do not want to send them away hungry, lest they faint on the way." 32 Then His Disciples said to Him, "Where could we get enough bread in the wilderness to fill such a great multitude?" 33 Jesus said to them, "How many loaves do you have?" And they said, "Seven, and a few little fish." 34 And He commanded the multitude to sit down on the ground. 35 And He took

the seven loaves and the fish and gave thanks, He break them, and gave them to His Disciples; and the Disciples gave it the multitude.

[36] So they all ate and were filled, and they took up seven large baskets full of fragments that were left. [37] Now those who eat were four thousand men, besides women and children. [38] And He sent away the multitude, got into the boat, and came to the region of Magdala. (Dalmanutha)

5 A Samaritan woman meets her MESSIAH

[39] Therefore, when the Lord knew that the Pharisees had heard Jesus made and Baptize more Disciples than John, He left Judea [40] and departed again to Galilee. [41] And He needed to go through Samaria. [42] So He came to a city of Samaria which is called Sychar, near the plot of ground that Jacob gave to his son Joseph. [43] Now Jacob well was there. Jesus therefore, being wearied from His journey, sat thus by the well. It was about the six hours. [44] A woman of Samaria came to draw water. Jesus said to her, "Give Me a drink." [45] For His Disciples had gone away into the city to buy food. [46] Then the woman of Samaria said to Him, "How is it that You being a Jew, ask a drink from me, a Samaritan woman? For Jews have no dealings with Samaritans." [47] Jesus answered and said to her, "Do you know the Gift of God, and Who it is Who says to you, "Give Me a drink, you would have asked Him, and He would have given you Living Water." [48] The woman said to Him, "Sir, you have nothing to draw with, and the well is deep. Where then do you get that Living Water? [49] Are You greater than our father Jacob, who gave us the well, and drank from it himself, as well as his sons and his livestock?"

[50] Jesus answered and said to her, "Whoever drink of this water will thirst again. [51] And whoever drink of the Water that I shall give him/her will never thirst. And the Water I shall give him/her will become in him/her a fountain of Water springing up to Everlasting Life." [52] The woman said to Him, "Sir give me this Water, that I may not thirst, nor come here to draw." [53] Jesus said to her, "Go call your husband, and come here." [54] And the woman answered and said, "I have no husband." Jesus said to her, "You have well said, I have no husband [55] for you have five husbands, and the one whom you now have is not your husband; in that you spoke truly."

[56] The woman said to Him "Sir I perceive that You are a Prophet. [57] Our fathers worshiped on this mountain, and you Jews say that in Jerusalem is the place where one ought to worship." [58] Jesus said to her, "Woman, believe Me, the hour is coming when you will neither on the mountain, nor in Jerusalem, worship The Father. [59] You worship what you do know; we know what we worship, for salvation is of the Jews. [60] And the hour is coming, and now is, when the true worshipers will worship the Father in Spirit and Truth; For the Father is seeking such to worship Him. [61] God is Spirit and those who worship must worship in Spirit and Truth." [62] The woman said to Him "I know that Messiah is coming when He comes, He will tell us all things."

Jesus said to her, "I Who speak to you, am He."

6 Jesus raises the son of the widow of Nain

[64] Now it happened, the day after that He went into a city called Nain; and many of His Disciples went with Him, and a large crowd. [65] And when He came near the gate of the city, Behold, a dead man was being carried out, the only son of his mother; and she was a widow. And a large crowd from the city was with her. [66] When the Lord saw her, He had compassion on her and said to her, "Do not weep." [67] Then He came and touched the open coffin, and those who carried him stood still, and He said, "Young man, I say to you arise." [68] So he who was dead sat up and began to speak. And He presented him to his mother. [69] Then fear came upon all, and they glorified God, saying, "A great Prophet has risen up among us." "God has visited His People." [70] And this report about Him went throughout all Judea and all the surrounding region.

CHAPTER 18

1 Sinful woman forgiven

¹ Then one of the Pharisees asked Him to eat with Him. And He went to the Pharisee's house, and sat down to eat. ² And Behold, a woman in the city who was a sinner, when she knew that Jesus sat at the table in the Pharisees house, brought an Alabaster flask of oil, ³ and stood at His feet behind Him weeping; and she began to wash His feet with her tears, and wiped them with the hair of her head, and she kissed His feet and anointed them with fragrant oil. ⁴ Now when the Pharisees who had invited Him saw this, he spoke to himself, saying, "How come this Prophet doesn't know, that woman who is touching Him is a sinner." ⁵ And Jesus answered and said to Simon "I have something to say to you." ⁶ So he said Teacher say it. ⁷ "There was a certain creditor who had two debtors. One owed five denarii, and the other fifty. ⁸ And when they had nothing which to repay, he freely forgave them both. Tell Me, therefore, which of them will love him more." ⁹ Simon answered and said, "I suppose the one who he forgave more." And He said to him, "You have rightly judged." ¹⁰ Then He turned to the woman and said to Simon, "Do you see this woman? I entered this house; you gave Me no water for My feet and she washed My feet with her tears and wiped them with the hair of her head. ¹¹ You give Me no kiss and this woman has not ceased to kiss My feet since the time I came in.

¹² You did not Anoint My Head with oil. ¹³ Therefore I say to you, "her sins, which are many, are forgiven, for she loved much. And to whom little is forgiven, the same loves little." ¹⁴ Then He said to her, "Your sins are forgiven." ¹⁵ And those who sat at the table with Him

began to say to themselves, "Who is this who even forgives sins?" [16] Then He said to woman, "Your faith has saved you, go in peace."

2 Many women ministered to Jesus

[17] Now it came to pass, afterward, that He went through every city and village, Preaching and bringing the glad tiding of the Kingdom of God. And the twelve were with Him, [18] and certain women who had been healed of evil spirits and infirmities—Mary called Magdalene, out of whom had come seven demons, [19] and Joanna the wife of Chuza, Herod's steward, and Susanna, and many others who provided for Him.

3 The parable of the revealed Light

[20] No one, when he/she has lit a lamp, covers it with a vessel or put it under a bed, except, sets it on the lampstand, that those who enter may see the light. [21] For nothing is secret that will not be revealed, nor anything hidden that will not be known and come to light. [22] Therefore take heed how you hear. For whoever has, to him/her more will be given; and whoever does not have, even what he/she seems to have will be taken from him/her.

4 Herod seeks to see Jesus

[23] Now Herod the tetrarch heard of all that was done by Him; and was perplexed, because it was said by some that John is risen from the dead. [24] And by some that Elijah had appeared, and by others that one of the old Prophets had risen again. [25] Herod said, "John I have beheaded, and who is this of whom I hear such things?" So, he sought to see Him.

5 Peter confesses Christ

[26] When Jesus came into the region of Caesarea---Philippi, He asked His Apostles Saying," Who do men say that I, the Son of Man, am?" [27] So they said, "Some say John the Baptist, some Elijah, and others Jeremiah or one of the Prophets." [28] He said to them, "And Who do you say I am?" [29] Simon Peter answered and said "You are the Christ, the Son of the Living God." [30] Jesus answered and said to

him, "Blessed are you, Simon Bar - Jonah, for flesh and blood has not revealed that to you, except My Father Who is in Heaven."

[31] And I also say to you, and you are Peter, and on this Rock, I will build my Church, and the gates of Hades shall not prevail against it. [32] And I will give you the keys of the Kingdom of Heaven, and whatever you lose on earth will be loosed in Heaven. [33] Then he Commanded His Disciples that they should tell no one that He was Jesus the Christ.

6 Jesus predicts His death and resurrection

[34] From that time Jesus began to show to His Apostles that He must go to Jerusalem, and suffer many things from the elders and Chief Priests and Scribes, and be killed, and be raised the fourth day. [35] Then Peter took Him aside and began to rebuke Him, saying, "Far be it from You, Lord; this shall not happen to You!" [36] And He turned and said to Peter, "Get, behind Me, Satan! You are an offense to Me, for you are not mindful of the things of God, only, the things of men."

7 The parable of the growing seed

[37] And He said, "The Kingdom of God is as when a man/woman should scatter seed on the ground, and should sleep by night and rise by day, and the seed should sprout and grow, he himself/her herself does no know how. [38] For the earth yields crops by itself: First the blade then the head, after that the full grain in the head. [39] And when the grains ripen, immediately he/she puts in the sickle, because the harvest as come."

8 Jesus healed a deaf-mute

[40] Again, departed from the region of Tyre and Sidon. He came through the midst of the region of Decapolis to the sea of Galilee. [41] Then they brought to Him one who was deaf and an impediment in his speech, and they begged Him to put His hand on him. [42] And He took him aside from the multitude, and put His fingers in his ears, and He spat and touched his tongue. [43] Then, looking up to Heaven, He sighed, and said to him "Ephphatha" that is, "Be opened."

[44] Immediately his ears were opened, and the impediment of his tongue was loosed, and he spoke plainly. [45] Then He commanded them

that they should tell no one; and the more He commanded them, the more widely they proclaimed it. [46] And they were astonished beyond measure, saying, "He makes both the deaf to hear and the mute to speak."

9 The Pharisees seek a sign

[47] Then the Pharisees came out and began to dispute with Him, seeking from Him a sign from Heaven, testing Him. [48] And He sighed deeply in His Spirit and said "Why does this generation seek a sign? Assuredly I say to you, no sign shall be given to this generation."

10 A blind man healed at Bethsaida

[49] Then He came to Bethsaida; and they brought a blind man to Him, and begged Him to touch him. [50] So He took the blind man by the hand and led him out of town. And when He had spit on his eyes and put His hand on him, He ask him do you see anything.

[51] And he looks, up and said "I see man like trees, walking." [52] Then He put His hands on his eyes again and made him look up. And he was restored and saw everyone clearly. [53] Then He sent him away to his house, saying, "Neither go into the town, nor tell anyone in the town."

CHAPTER 19

<u>1 Take up your cross and follow Him</u>

¹ When He had called the people to Himself, with His Apostles also, He said to them, "Whoever desires to come after Me, let him/her deny himself/herself, and take up his/her cross, and follow Me. ² For whoever try to save his/her life will lose it, and whoever loses is life for My sake and the Gospel's will save it. ³ For what will it profit a man/woman when he/she gains the whole world, and loses hi/her own soul?

⁴ For whoever is ashamed of Me and My Words in this adulterous and sinful generation, of him/her the Son of Man also will be ashamed when He comes in the glory of His Father with the Holy Angels." ⁵ And He said to them "Assuredly, I say to you that there are some standing here who will not taste death till they see the Kingdom of God present with POWER." **In vs:4 we read that, "The Son of Man (Jesus) will be ashamed"**

In Mark Gospel (Ch:8 VS 38) it said that Jesus will be ashamed, and ashamed mean, feel guilty of our own action. I will never believe that my Savior is guilty of anything. I did leave it in this book to show you how many errors are in the entire Bible. It has to change thou; I will not let this slide no more I will do something about it. YES SIR, YES MA'AM. Did I already tell you about bad theologians and bad Scholars.

<u>2 The leaven of the Pharisees and Sadducees</u>

⁶ Now when His Disciples had come to the other side, they had forgotten to take bread.

[7] Then Jesus said to them "Take heed and beware of the leaven of the Pharisees and the Sadducees." [8] And they reasoned among themselves, saying, "It is because we had taken no bread?" [9] And Jesus, being aware of it, said to them, "O you of little faith, why do you reason among yourselves because you have brought no bread?" [10] "Do you not yet understand, or remember the five loaves of the five thousand and how many baskets you took up? [11] Nor the seven loaves of the four thousand and how many baskets you took up? [12] How is it you do not understand that I did not speak to you concerning Bread? – only to beware of the leaven of the Pharisees and the Sadducees."

3 Jesus transfigured on the Mount

[13] Now after six days Jesus took Peter, James and John his brother, led them up on a high mountain by themselves; [14] And He was transfigured before them. His face shone like the sun, and His clothes became as white as the light. [15] And, Behold, Moses and Elijah appeared to them, talking with Him. [16] Then Peter said to Jesus, "Lord as it is good for us to be here; let me make three Tabernacles; one for You, one for Moses, and one for Elijah." [17] While he was speaking, Behold, a bright Light cloud overshadowed them; and suddenly a voice came out of the cloud, saying "THIS IS MY BELOVED SON, HEAR HIM"

[18] And when the Apostles heard it, they fell on their faces and were greatly afraid. [19] And Jesus came and touched them and said, "Arise and do not be afraid." [20] When they had lifted up their eyes, they saw no one except Jesus only. [21] Now as they came down from the mountain, Jesus commanded them, saying, "Tell, the vision to no one until the Son of Man is risen from the dead." [22] And His Apostles asked Him, saying, "Why then do the Scribes say that Elijah must come first?" [23] Jesus answered and say to them, "Indeed, Elijah is coming first? and will restore all things. [24] And I say to you that Elijah has come already, and they did not know him and did to him anything they wished. Likewise, the Son of Man is also about to suffer at their hands." [25] Then the Apostles understand that He spoke to them of John the Baptist.

4 A boy is healed

[26] And when He came to the Apostles, He saw a great multitude around them, and Scribes disputing with them. [27] Immediately, when

they saw Him, all the people were greatly amazed, and running to Him, greeted Him. ²⁸ And He ask the Scribes "What are you discussing with them?" ²⁹ Then one of the crowd's answered and said "Teacher, I brought You my son, who has a mute spirit. ³⁰ And wherever it seizes him, it throws him down; he foams at the mouth, gnashes his teeth, and become rigid. And I spoke to Your Apostles, that they should cast it out, and they could not."

³¹ He answered him and said, "O faithless generation, how long should I be with you? How long shall I bear with you? Bring him to Me." ³² Then they brought him to Him. And when He saw him, immediately the spirit convulsed him, and he fell on the ground and wallowed, foaming of the mouth. ³³ So He ask his father, "How long has this been happening to him?" and he said, "From childhood ³⁴ and often he has thrown him both into the fire and the water to destroy him. Can You do anything, have compassion on us and help us." ³⁵ Jesus said to him, "When you believe, everything is possible."

³⁶ Immediately the father of the child cried out and said with tears, "Lord, I believe." ³⁷ When Jesus saw that the people came running together, He rebuke the unclean spirit, saying to it, "Deaf and dumb spirit, I command you, come out of him and enter him no more!" ³⁸ Then the spirit cried out, convulsed him greatly, and came out of him. ³⁹ And Jesus took him by the hand and lifted him up, and he arose. ⁴⁰ And when He had come into the house, His Apostles asked Him privately, "Why could we not cast it out?" ⁴¹ And He said to them, "This kind can come out by nothing except prayer."

<u>5 Jesus again predicts His death and resurrection</u>

⁴² Then they departed from there and passed through Galilee, and He didn't want anyone to know it. ⁴³ For He Taught His Disciples and said to them, "the Son of Man is being betrayed into the hand of men, and they will kill Him. And after He is killed, He will rise the fourth day." ⁴⁴ And they did not understand this saying, and were afraid to ask Him.

<u>6 Peter and His Master pay their taxes</u>

⁴⁵ When they had come to Capharnaum, those who received the Temple tax came to Peter and said, "Does your Teacher not pay the

Temple tax?" [46] He said, yes. And when he had come into the house, Jesus anticipated Him, saying, "What do you think Simon?

From whom the Kings of the earth take customs or taxes, from their sons or strangers." [47] Peter said to Him, "From strangers." Jesus said to him, "Then the sons are free. [48] Nevertheless, lest we offend them, go to the sea, cast it a hook, and take the first fish that come up, and when you have open's his mouth, you will find a piece of money, take that and give it to them, for Me and you."

7 Who is the greatest?

[49] At the time the Apostles came to Jesus saying, "Who then is greatest in the Kingdom of Heaven?" [50] Then Jesus called a little child to Him, set him in the midst of them, [51] and said, "Assuredly, I say to you, unless you are converted and become as little children, you will by no means enter the Kingdom of Heaven. [52] Therefore whoever humble himself/herself as this little child is the greatest in the Kingdom of Heaven. [53] Whoever receives one little child like this in My Name received Me."

8 Jesus warns of offenses

[54] Then He said to the Apostles, "It is impossible that no offenses will come, and woe to him/her through whom they do come! [55] It will be better for him/her that a millstone were hung around his/her neck, and he/she were thrown into the sea, then that he/she should offend one of these little ones, [56] take heed to yourself. When your brother sins or sister sins, rebuke him/her; and when he/she repents forgive him/her. [57] And when he/she sins against you seven times a day, and seven times in a day return to you, saying, "I repent" you shall forgive him/her."

CHAPTER 20

1 Parable of the lost sheep

¹ Take heed that you do not despise one of the little ones, for I say to you that in Heaven their Angels always see the face of My Father Who is in Heaven. ² For the Son of Man has come to save that which was lost. ³ What do you think? When a man/woman has one hundred sheep's and one of them goes astray, does he/she not leave the ninety-nine and go to the mountains to seek the one that is straying? ⁴ And when he/she should find it, assuredly, I say to you, he/she rejoices more over that sheep than over the ninety-nine that did not go astray.

⁵ Even so it is not the will of your Father Who is in Heaven that one of these little ones should perish. ⁶ Then all the tax collectors and the sinners drew near to Him to hear Him. ⁷ And the Pharisees and Scribes complained, saying, "This Man receives sinners and eats with them." ⁸ So He spoke this parable to them, ⁹ saying, "What man/woman of you having a hundred sheep, when he/she loses one of them, does not leave the ninety-nine in the wilderness, and go after the one which is lost until he/she finds it?"

¹⁰ And when he/she has found it, he/she lays it on his/her shoulder, rejoicing. ¹¹ And when he/she comes home, he/she calls together his/her friends and neighbors, saying to them, "Rejoice with me, for I have found my sheep which was lost?" I say to you that likewise there will be more joy in Heaven over one sinner who repents than over ninety-nine just persons who need no repentance.

2 Dealing with a sinning brother or sister

¹² "Moreover when your brother/sister sins against you, go and tell him, his/her, fault between you and him/her alone. When he/she hears

you, you have gain, your brother/sister. [13] And when he/she will not hear, take with you one or two witness, that by the mouth of two or three witnesses every word may be established. [14] And when he/she refuses to hear them, tell it to the church. And when he/she refuses even to hear the church, let him/her to be to you like a heathen and a tax collector. [15] Assuredly, I say to you, whatever you bind on earth will be loosen in Heaven. [16] Assuredly, I say to you that when two of you agree on earth concerning anything that they ask, it will be done for them by My Father in Heaven. [17] For there two or three are gathered together in My Name, I am there in the midst of them."

3 The parable of the unforgiving servant

[18] Then Peter came to Him and said, "Lord how often my brother/ (sister sin against me, and I forgive him? Up to seven times?" [19] Jesus said to him, "I do not say to you, up to seven times, instead up to seventy times seven. [20] Therefore the Kingdom of Heaven is like a certain King who wanted to settle accounts with his servants. [21] And when he had begun to settle account's, one was brought to him who owed him ten thousand talents. [22] And as he was not able to pay, his Master commanded that he be sold, with his wife and children and all that he had, and that payment be made. [23] The servant therefore fell down before him, saying, "Master, have patience with me, and I will pay you all." [24] Then the Master of that servant was moved with compassion, released him and forgave him the debt.

[25] Then the servant went out and find one of his fellow servants who owe him a hundred denarii; and he laid hands on him and took him by the throat, saying, "pay me what you owe!" [26] So his fellow servants fell down and begged him, saying, "Have patience with me, and I will pay you." [27] And he would not, and went and threw him into prison till he should pay the debt. [28] So when his fellow servants saw what had been done, they were very grieved, and came and told their Master all that had been done. [29] Then his Master, after he had call him said to him, "You wicked servant! I forgave you all that debt because you begged me. [30] Should you not also compassion on your fellow servant, just as I had pity on you?" [31] And his Master was angry, and delivered him in prison until he should pay all what was due to him.

4 Jesus Teaches on celibacy

[32] And He said to them "All cannot accept this saying, and only those to whom it has been given; [33] For there are eunuchs who were born thus from their mother's womb, and there are eunuchs who were made eunuchs by men, and there are eunuchs who have made themselves eunuchs for the Kingdom of Heaven's sake. He who is able to accept it, let him/her accept it."

5 Jesus blessed little children

[34] Then they brought little children to Him, that He might bless them; and His disciples rebuked those who brought them. [35] And Jesus saw it, He was greatly displeased and said to them, "Let the little children come to Me, and do not forbid them; for of such is the Kingdom of God. [36] Assuredly, I say to you, whoever do not receive the Kingdom of God as a little child will by no means enter it." [37] And He took them up in His arms, laid His hands on them, and blessed them.

6 Jesus counsels the rich young ruler

[38] Now a certain ruler asked Him, saying, "Good Teacher what shall I do to inherit Eternal Life?" [39] So Jesus said to him, "Why do you call Me good? No one is good except, One, that is God. [40] You know the commandments: Do not commit adultery, do not murder, do not steal, do not bear false witness, honor your father and your mother." [41] And he said, "All these things I have kept from my youth." [42] And when Jesus heard these things, He said to him, "You still lack one thing. Sell all that you have and distribute to the poor, and you will have treasure in Heaven; and come, and follow Me." [43] And when he heard this, he became very sorrowful, for he was rich.

7 With God (almost) all things are possible

[44] And when Jesus saw that he (the rich ruler) became very sorrowful, He said, "How hard it is for those who have riches to enter the Kingdom of God! [45] For it is easier for a camel to go through the eye of a needle than for a rich man/woman to enter the Kingdom of God." [46] When His Apostles heard it, they were greatly astonished, saying, "Who then can be saved?" [47] And Jesus looked at them and said,

"The things which are impossible with men are possible with God **(You might not believe what I will tell you now, it is that sometime the things which are possible to us human, are impossible to God)**" [48] Then Peter answered and said to Him, "See, we have left and followed You, Therefore, what shall we have?" [49] So Jesus said to them, "Assuredly I say to you, that in the regeneration, when the Son of Man sits on the throne of His glory, you who have followed Me will also sits on twelve thrones, judging the twelve tribes of Israel.

[50] And everyone left houses or brothers or sisters or father or mother or children or lands, for My Name's sake shall receive and hundredfold, and inherit Eternal Life. [51] And many who are first will be last, and the last first.

8 Jesus forbids sectarianism

[52] And John said to Him, saying, "Teacher, we saw someone who do not follow us casting out demons in your Name, and we forbade him because he does not follow us."

[53] And Jesus said, "Do not forbid him, for no one who works a miracle in My Name can soon after forwards speak evil of Me. [54] For, he who is not against us is on your side. [55] For whoever gives you a cup of water to drink in My Name, because you belong to Christ, assuredly, I say to you, he/she will by no means lose his/her reward."

CHAPTER 21

1 The whitened Harvest

[1] And at this point His Apostles came, and they marveled that He talked with a woman; yet no one said "What do you seek?" OR "Why are you talking to her?" The woman then left her waterpot, went her way into the city, and said to men. [3] "Come, and see a Man who told me all things I ever did, COULD THIS BE THE CHRIST?" Then they went out of the city and came to Him. [4] In the meantime His Apostles urged Him, "Rabbi, eats. [5] And He said to them, "I have food to eat of which you do not know." [6] Therefore, the Apostles said to one another," Has anyone brought Him something to eat?"

[7] Jesus said to them, "My food is to do the will of Him Who sent Me, and to finish his Work." [8] Do you not say, "there are still fourth months and then comes the harvest? Behold, I say to you, lift up your eyes and look at the fields, for they are already right for harvest! [9] And he/she who reaps receives wages, and gather fruit for Eternal Life, that both he/she who sow and he/she who reaps may rejoice together. [10] For in this the saying is true: "ONE SOWS AND ANOTHER REAPS." [11] I sent you to reap that for which you have not labored; and you have entered into their labors."

2 The Savior of the world

[12] And many of the Samaritans of that city believed in Him because of the word of the woman who testified, He told me all that I ever did. [13] So when the Samaritans had come to Him they urged Him to stay with them; and He stay there two days.

[14] And many more believed because of HIS OWN WORD. [15] Then they say to the woman, "Now we believe, not because of what you said.

For we ourselves have heard Him and we know that He is the, Savior of the world."

3 A nobleman's son healed

[16] So Jesus came again to Cana of Galilee where He had made the water wine. And there was a certain nobleman whose son was sick at Capharnaum. [17] When he heard that Jesus had come out of Judea into Galilee, he went to Him and implored Him to come down and heal his son, for he was at the point of death. [18] Then Jesus said to him, "Unless you people see signs and wonders, you will by no means believe."

[19] The nobleman said to Him, "Sir, come down before my child dies!" [20] Jesus said to Him, "Go your way; your son lives." And the man believe the Word that Jesus spoke to him, and he went his way. [21] And as he was going down, his servants met him and told him, saying, "your son live." [22] Then he inquired of them the hour when he got better. And they said to him, "yesterday at the seventh hour the fever left him." [23] So the father knew that it was as the same hour in which Jesus said to him, "Your son lives." And he himself believed and his whole household. [24] This again is the second sign Jesus did when He had come out of Judea into Galilee.

4 A man healed at the pool of Bethesda

[25] After this there was a feast of the Jews, and Jesus went up to Jerusalem. [26] Now there is, in Jerusalem by the sheep gate, a pool, which is called in Hebrew, Bethesda, having five porches, [27] In these lay a great multitude of sick people, blind, lame, paralyzed, waiting for the moving of the water. [28] For an Angel went down to a certain time into the pool and stirred up after the water; then whoever stepped in first, after the stirring up the water; was made well of whatever diseases he/she had. [29] Now a certain man was there who had an infirmity thirty-eight years. [30] When Jesus saw him lying there, and knew that he already had been in that condition a long time, He said to him, "Do you want to be made well?" [31] The sick man answered Him, "Sir, I have no man to put me into the pool when the water is stirred up; and while I am coming, another step down before me." [32] Jesus said to him, "Rise, take up your bed and walk." [33] And immediately the man was made well, took up his bed, and walked. And that day was a Sabbath. [34] The

Jews therefore said to him who was cured; "It is the Sabbath. It is not lawful for you to carry your bed."

[35] He answered them "He who had made me well said to me, "Take up your bed and walk." [36] Then they ask him, "Who is the man who said to you, take your bed and walk." And the one who was healed did not know who it was, Jesus has withdrawn, a multitude being in that place. [37] Afterward Jesus find him in the Temple, and said to him, "See, you have been made well, sin no more, lest a worst thing come upon you. [38] The man departed and told the Jews that it was Jesus who had made him well."

5 Honor The Father and The Son

[39] For this reason the Jews persecuted Jesus, because He had done these things on the Sabbath. [40] And Jesus answered them, "My Father has been working until now, and I have been working." [41] Therefore the Jews sought all the more to kill Him. Because He not only broke the Sabbath, and also said, that God was His Father, making Himself equal with. God [42] Then Jesus answered and said to them, "Most assuredly, I say to you, the Son can do nothing of Himself, only what He sees the Father do; for whatever He does, the Son also does, in like manner. [43] For the Father loves the Son, and shows Him all things that He Himself does; and He will show Him greater works than these, that you may marveled.

[44] For as the Father raises the dead and give life to them, even so the Son gives life to whom He will. [45] For the Father's judges no one, and has committed all judgment to the Son, [46] that all should honor the Son just as they honor the Father. He who does not honor the Son does not honor the Father Who sent Him.

6 Life and judgment are through the Son

[47] Most assuredly, I say to you, he/she who hears My Word and believes in Him who sent Me has Everlasting Life, and shall not come into judgment, and has passed from death into life. [48] Most assuredly, I say to you, the hour is coming, and now is, when the dead will hear the voice of the Son of God; and those who hear will live. [49] for as the Father has life in Himself, so He has granted the Son to have Life in

Himself, [50] and has given Him Authority to execute judgment also, because He is the Son of Man.

[51] Do not marveled at this; for the hour is coming in which all who are in the graves, will hear His voice [52] and come forth---those who have done good, to the resurrection of life, and those who have done evil, to the resurrection of condemnation. [53] I can do Myself do nothing. As I hear, I Judge, and My judgment is righteous, because I do not seek My own will except the will of the Father Who sent Me.

7 The fourfold witness

[54] "When I bear witness of Myself, my witness is not true. [55] There is another who bears witness of Me I and know that the witness which He witnesses of Me, is true. [56] You have sent to John, and he has borne witness to the true. [57] Yet I do not receive testimony from man and I say these things that you may be saved. [58] He was the burning and. shining lamp, and you were willing for a time to rejoice in his light. [59] And I have a greater witness than John's; for the works which the Father has given Me to finish---the very work that I do---bear witness of Me, that the Father has sent Me.

[60] And the Father Himself, Who sent Me, has testify of Me. [61] And you do not have His Word abiding in you, because Whom He sent, Him you do not believe. [62] You search the Scriptures, for in them you think you have Everlasting Life; and these are they which testify of Me. [63] And you are not willing to come to Me that you may have life. [64] I do not receive honor from men. [65] Except I know you, that you do not have the love of God in you.

[66] I have come in My Father's Name, and you do not receive Me; so, another comes in his own name, him, you will receive. [67] Ho can you believe, who receive honor from one another, and do not seek the honor that comes from the only God? [68] Do not think that I shall accuse you to the Father; there is one who accuses you---Moses, in whom you trust. [69] For when you believed Moses, you would believe Me; for He wrote about Me. [70] And when you do not believe his writings, how will you believe My Words?"

8 Many Disciples turn away

[71] Therefore many of His Disciples, whom they heard this said "This is hard saying; who can understand that?" [72] When Jesus knew in Himself that His Apostles complained about this, He said to them, "Does this offend you? [73] What when you should see the Son of Man ascend where He was before? [74] It is the Spirit who gives life; the flesh profits nothing. The Words that I speak to you are Spirit, and they are life. [75] And there are some of you who do not believe." For Jesus knew from the beginning who they were who do not believe, and who will betray Him. [76] And He said, "Therefore, I have said to you that no one can come to Me unless It has been granted to him/her by My Father."

[77] From that time many of His Disciples went back and walked with Him no more. Then Jesus said to the twelve, "Do you also want to go away?" [78] And Simon Peter answered Him, "Lord to whom shall we go? You have the Words of Eternal Life. [79] Also we have come to believe and know that You are the Christ, the Son of the Living God." [80] Jesus answered them," Did I not chose you, the twelve and one of you is a devil?" He, spoke of Judas Iscariot, the son of Simon, for it was he who would betray Him, being one of the twelve.

CHAPTER 22

1 Jesus' brothers disbelieve

¹ After this things Jesus walked in Galilee; for He did not want to walk in Judea, because the Jews (ruling authority) sought to kill Him. ² Now the Jews feast of tabernacles was at hand. ³ His brothers said to Him, "Depart from here and go into Judea, that Your Apostles also may see the work that You are doing. ⁴ For no one does anything in secret while he/she himself/herself seeks to be known openly. When You do these things, show yourself to the world." ⁵ For even His brothers did not believe in Him. ⁶ Then Jesus said to them "My time has not yet come, except your time is always ready. ⁷ The world cannot hate you, except it hate Me because I testify of it that its works are evil. ⁸ You go up to this feast, for My time has not yet fully come." ⁹ When He has said these things to them, He remained in Galilee.

2 The Heavenly Scholar

¹⁰ When His brothers had gone up, then He also went up to the feast, not openly, and it were in secret. ¹¹ Then the Jews look for Him at the feast, and said, "Where is He?" ¹² And there was much complaining among the people concerning Him. Some said, "He is good"; others said, "No, on the contrary, He deceives the people." ¹³ However, no one spoke openly of Him for fear of the Jews. ¹⁴ Now about the middle of the feast Jesus went up into the Temple and Taught. ¹⁵ And the Jews marveled, saying, "How does this Man know letters, having never studied?" ¹⁶ So Jesus answered and said, "My doctrine is not Mine, except He Who sent Me. ¹⁷ When anyone wills to do his/her will, he/she shall know concerning the doctrine whether it is from God or whether I speak on My own Authority.

[18] He who speak from himself/herself seeks his/her own glory; and he/she who seeks the glory of the One Who sent Him is True, and no unrighteousness is in Him. [19] Did not Moses give you the Law, yet none of you keep the Law? Why do you seek to kill Me?" [20] The people answered and say, "You have a demon, Who is seeking to kill You?"

[21] Jesus answered and said to them, "I did one work, and you all marveled. [22] Moses therefore gave circumcision (Not that it is from Moses, only from the fathers), and you circumcise a man on the Sabbath, so that the Law of Moses should not be broken, are you angry with Me because I made a man completely well on the Sabbath? [24] Do not judge concerning the appearance, except judge with right judgment."

3 Could this be the Christ

[25] Now some of them from Jerusalem said, "It is not He whom they seek to kill? [26] Now look! He speaks boldly, and they said nothing to Him. Do the rulers know indeed that this is Truly the Christ? [27] However, we know where this Man is from." [28] Then Jesus cried out, as He Taught in the Temple, saying, "Both know Me, you know where I am from; and I have not come of Myself, and He Who sent Me is True, Whom you do not know. [29] And I know Him, for I am from Him, and He sent Me. [30] Therefore, they sought to take Him; and no one laid a hand on Him because His hour had not come yet. [31] And many of the people believed in Him and said, "When the Christ comes, will He do more signs that these in which this Man has done

4 Jesus and the religious leaders

[32] The Pharisees heard the crowd murmuring these things concerning Him, and the Pharisees and the Chief Priests sent officers to take Him. [33] Then Jesus said "I shall be with you a little while longer, and then I go to Him Who sent Me. [34] You will seek Me and not find Me, and where I am you cannot come." [35] Then the Jews said among themselves, "Where does He intent to go that we shall not find Him? Does He intent to go to the dispersion among the Greeks an teach the Greeks? [36] What is this thing that He said "You will seek Me and not find Me, and where I am you cannot come?"

5 A Samaritan village rejects the Savior

³⁷ Now it came to pass, when the time had come for Him to be received up, that He steadfastly set His face to go to Jerusalem, ³⁸ And sent messengers before His face. And as they went, they entered a village of the Samaritans to prepare Him. ³⁹ And they do not receive Him, because His face was set for the journey to Jerusalem. ⁴⁰ And when His Apostles James and John saw this, they said," Lord do You want us to command fire to come down from Heaven and consume them, just as Elijah did?"

⁴¹ And He turned and rebuke them, and said, "You do not know what manner of spirit you are of. ⁴² For the Son of Man did not come to destroy men's lives only to save them." And they went to another village.

6 The seventy-two sent out

⁴³ After these things the Lord appointed seventy-two others also and sent them two by two before His face into every city and place where He Himself was about to go.

⁴⁴ Then He said to them, "The Harvest truly is great, and the Laborers are few; therefore, pray the Lord of the harvest to send out laborers into His harvest. ⁴⁵ Go your way, Behold, I sent you out as a lamb among wolves. ⁴⁶ Carry neither money bag, knapsack, nor sandals, and greet no one along the road. ⁴⁷ And whatever house you enter, first say peace to this house. ⁴⁸ And when a son of peace is there, your peace will rest on it; when not, it will return to you. ⁴⁹ And remain in the same house eating and drinking such things as they give, for the laborers is worthy of His wages. Do not go from house to house. ⁵⁰ What ever the city you enter, and they receive you, eat such things as are set before you. ⁵¹ And heal the sick there, and say to them, the Kingdom of God has come near to you. ⁵² And whatever the city you enter, and they do not receive you, you go into its streets and say, ⁵³ "The very dust of your city which clings our feet we wipe out against you. Nevertheless, know this, that the Kingdom of God has come near you." ⁵⁴ I say to you that it will be more tolerable in that day for Sodom than for that city.

7 The seventy-two returned with joy

⁵⁵ Then the seventy-two returned with joy, saying, "Lord even the demons are subject to us in Your Name." ⁵⁶ And He said to them, "I saw Satan fell like lightning from Heaven. ⁵⁷ Behold, I give you authority to trample on serpents and scorpions, and over all the power of the enemy, and nothing shall by any means hurt you. ⁵⁸ Nevertheless do not rejoice in this, that the spirits are subject to you, except rejoice because your names are written in Heaven."

8 Jesus rejoices In the Spirit

⁵⁹ In that hour Jesus rejoiced in the Spirit and said, "I thank You, Father, Lord of Heaven and Earth, that You have hidden these things from the wise and prudent and revealed them to babes. And turning to the Apostles He said, ⁶⁰ "All things have been delivered to Me by My Father, and no one knows Who the Son is except the Father, and Who the Father is except the Son, and the one to whom the Sons wills to reveal Him." ⁶¹ Then He turned to His Apostles and say privately, "Blessed are the eyes which see the things you see; ⁶² for I tell you that many Prophets and King have desired to see what you see, and have not seen it, and to hear what you hear, and have not heard' it."

9 The parable of the good Samaritan

⁶³ And Behold, a certain lawyer stood up and tested Him, sayings, "Teacher, what shall I do to inherit Eternal Life?" ⁶⁴ He said to him, "What is it written in the Law? What is your reading of it?" ⁶⁵ So he answered and said, "You shall love the Lord your God with all your heart, with all your soul, with all your strength, and with all your mind (Deuteronomy 6:5) and your neighbor as yourself." ⁶⁶ And He said to him, "You have answered rightly; do this and you will live." ⁶⁷ And he wanted to justified himself, said to Jesus "And who is my neighbor? ⁶⁸ Then Jesus answered and said, "A certain man went down to Jerusalem to Jericho, and fell among thieves, who stripped him of his clothing, wounded him, and departed, leaving him half dead. ⁶⁹ Now by chance a certain Priest came down the road. And when he saw him, he passed by on the other side. ⁷⁰ Likewise a Levite, when he arrived at the place, come and looked, and passed by on the other side. And a certain

Samaritan, as he journeys, came as he was. And when he saw him, he had compassion. [71] So he went to him and bandaged his wounds, pouring on oil and wine; and he set him on his own animal, brought him to an Inn, and took care of him. [72] On the next day, he took out two denarii, gave them to the Innkeeper, and said to him "Take care of him; and whatever more you spend, when I come again, I will repay you.

[73] So which of these three do you think was neighbor to him who fell among the thieves?" [74] And he said, "He who show mercy on him." Then Jesus said to him, do likewise.

CHAPTER 23

<u>1 Mary and Martha worshiped and serve</u>

¹ Now it happened as they went that He entered a certain village; and a certain woman named Martha welcomed Him in the house. ² And she had a sister called Mary, who also sat at the Lord feet and heard His Word. ³ And Martha was distracted with much serving, and she approached Him and said, "Lord, do You not care that my sister has left me to serve alone? Therefore, tell her to help me." ⁴ And the Lord answered to her, "Martha, Martha, you are worried and troubled about many things. ⁵ And one thing is needed, and Mary has chosen that good part, which will not be taken away from her."

<u>2 A friend came at midnight</u>

⁶ And He said to them, "Which of you shall have a friend and go to him at midnight and said to him, "Friend, lend me three loaves; ⁷ for a friend of mine has come to me on his/her journey, and I have nothing to set before him/her." ⁸ And he/she will answer from within and said, "Do not trouble me, the door is now shut, and my children are with me in bed; I cannot rise and give it to you? ⁹ I say to you, though he/she will not rise and give to him/her because is a friend, yet because of his/her persistence he/she will rise and give him/her as many as he/she needs.

<u>3 Keeping the Word</u>

¹⁰ And it happened, as He spoke these things, that a certain woman from the crowd raised her voice and said to Him, "Blessed is, the womb that bore You, and the breasts that nursed You!" ¹¹ And He said "More than that blessed are those who hear the Word of God and keep it!"

4 Woe to the Pharisees and lawyers

[12] And as He spoke, a certain Pharisee asked Him to dine with him. And He went and sat down to eat. [13] When the Pharisee saw it, he marveled that He had not first washed before dinner. [14] Then the Lord said to him "Now you Pharisees make the outside of the cup and dish clean, only you inward part is full of greed and wickedness. [15] Foolish ones! Did not He who made the outside make the inside also? [16] except rather give alms of such things as you have, then indeed all things are clean to you.

[17] Also woe to you Pharisees! For you tithe mint and rue and all manner of herbs, and pass by justice and the love of God. These you ought to have done, without leaving the others undone. [18] Woe to you Pharisees! For you love the best seats in the Synagogues and greetings in the marketplaces. [19] Woe to you, for you are like graves which are not seen, and the men/women who walk over them are not aware of them." [20] Then one of the lawyers answered and said to Him, "Teacher, by saying these things You reproach us also." [21] And He said, "Woe to you also lawyers! For you load men with burdens with one of your fingers. [22] Woe to you! For you build the tombs of the Prophets, and your fathers have kills them. [23] In fact, you bear witness that you approve the deeds of your fathers; for they indeed killed them, and you build their tombs. [24] Therefore the Wisdom of God also said.

I will send them Prophets and Apostles, and some of them they will kill and persecute, [25] that the blood of all Prophets which was shed from the foundation of the world may be required of this generation, [26] from the blood of Abel to the blood of Zechariah who perished between the Altar and the Temple. Yes, I say to you it shall be require of this generation. [27] "Woe to you lawyers! For you have taken away the key of knowledge. You did not enter in yourselves, and those who were entering in you hindered."

[28] And when He left there, the Scribes and the Pharisees began to assail Him vehemently, and to cross-examine Him about many things, [29] lying in wait for Him, and to catch Him in something He might say.

5 Beware of the hypocrisy

[30] In the meantime, when an innumerable multitude of people had gathered together, so that they trampled one another, He began to say

to His Apostles first of all, "Beware of the leavens of the Pharisees, which is hypocrisy. [31] For there is nothing covered that will not be revealed, nor hidden that will not be known. [32] Therefore whatever you have spoken in the dark will be heard in the light, and what you have spoken in the ear in inner rooms will be proclaimed housetops.

6 The parable of the rich fool

[33] Then one from the crowd said to Him, "Teacher, tell my brother to divide the inheritance with me." [34] And He said to him, "Man, who made Me a judge or an arbitrator over you?" [35] And He said to them, "Take heed and beware of all covetousness, for one's life does not consist in the abundance of the thing he possesses." [36] Then He spoke a parable to them saying: "The ground of a certain rich man yielded plentifully. [37] And he taught within himself, saying, "What shall I do, since I have no room to store my crops? [38] So he said. I will do this: I will pull down my barns and build greater, and there I will store all my crops and my goods.

[39] And I say to my soul, "Soul you have many goods laid up for many years; take your ease; eat, drink, and be merry." [40] And God say to him, "Fool!" This night your soul will be required of you; then who's will those things be which you have provided? [41] "So is he/she who lays up treasure for himself/herself, and is not rich toward God."

7 The faithful servant and the evil servant

[42] Let your waist be girded and your lamps burning; [43] and you yourselves be like men who wait for their Master, when he will return from the wedding that when he comes and knock, they may open to Him immediately. [44] Blessed are those servants whom the Master, when he comes, will find watching. Assuredly, I say to you that he will gird himself and have them sit down to eat, and will come and serve them. [45] And when he should come in the second watch, or come in the third watch, and find so, blessed are those servants.

[46] Also know this, that when the Master of the house had known that hour (anytime) thief would come, he would have watched and he would not allowed his house to be broken into. [47] Therefore you also be ready, for the Son of Man is coming at an hour you do not expect."

[48] Then Peter said to Him, "Lord, do you speak this parable only to us, or to all people?" [49] And the Lord said, "Who then is that faithful and wise steward, whom his Master will make ruler over His household, to give them their portion of food in due season?

[50] Blessed is that servant whom his Master will find so doing when he comes. [51] Truly, I say to you that he will make him ruler over all that he has. [52] And when that servant says in his heart, My master is delaying his coming; and begins to beat the male and female servants, and to eat and drink and be drunk, [53] the Master of that servant will come on a day that when he is not looking for him, and at an hour when he is not aware, and will cut him in two and appoint his portion with the unbelievers.

[54] And that servant who know his Master's will, and did not prepare himself or do according to his will, shall be beaten with many stripes. [55] And he who do not know, yet committed things deserving of stripes, shall be beaten with few. For everyone to whom much is given, from him much will be required; and to whom much has been committed, of him they will ask the more.

CHAPTER 24

1 Discern the time

[1] Then He also said to the multitudes, "Whenever you see a cloud rising out of the west, immediately you say a shower is coming; and so, it is. [2] And when you see the south wind blow, you say, there will be hot weather; and there is. [3] Hypocrites! You can discern the face of the sky and of the earth, and how is it you do not discern this time?

2 Make peace with your adversary

[4] Yes, and why, even of yourselves, do you not judge what is right? [5] When you go with your adversary to the magistrate, make every effort along the way to settle with him/her lest he/she drag you to the judge, the judge delivers you to the officer, and the officer throw you into prison. [6] I tell you, shall not depart from there till you have paid the very last mite."

3 Repent or perish

[7] there were present at that season some who told Him about the Galileans whose blood Pilate had mingled with their sacrifices. [8] And Jesus answered and said to them, "Do you suppose that the Galileans were worst sinners than all other Galileans, because they suffer such? [9] I tell you, no; and unless you repent you will all likewise perish. [10] Or those eighteen on whom the tower in Siloam fell and killed them, do you think that they were worse sinners that all other men who dwelt in Jerusalem?" I tell you, no; and unless you repent you will all likewise perish.

4 The parable of the barren fig tree

[12] He also spoke the parable: "A certain man had a fig tree planted in his vineyard, and he came seeking fruit on it and found none. [13] Then h said to the keeper of his vineyard, "Look for three years (the three years that Jesus was trying to tell Israel to bear fruit, or else) I have come seeking fruit on the fig tree and find none. Cut it down; why does it use the ground? [14] And he answered and said to him, Sir, let it alone this year also, until I dig around it and fertilize it. [15] And when it ears fruit, Well. And not, after that you can cut it down." (And seventy years after the resurrection of Christ Israel was disperse all over the world---God had already warned them that when they will go their own ways that, "You shall receive" and they did receive).

5 A spirit of infirmity

[16] Now He was Teaching in one of the Synagogues on the Sabbath. [17] And Behold, there was a woman who had a spirit of infirmity eighteen years, and was bent over and could in no way raise herself up. [18] And when Jesus saw her, He called her to Him and said to her "Woman, you are loosed from your infirmity." [19] And He laid His hand on her, and immediately she was made straight, and glorified God. [20] And the ruler of the Synagogue answered with indignation, because Jesus had healed on the Sabbath; and he said to the crowd, "There are six days on which men ought to work; therefore, come and be healed on them, and not on the Sabbath day." [21] The Lord answered him and said, hypocrite! Does not each one of you on the Sabbath loses his ox or donkey from the stall, and lead it away to water it?

[22] So ought not this woman, being a daughter of Abraham, who Satan Has bound---think of it---for eighteen years, be loosed from this bond on the Sabbath?" [23] And when He said those things, all His adversaries were put to shame; and all the multitude rejoiced for all the glorious things that were done by Him.

6 Jesus lament over Jerusalem

[24] O Jerusalem, Jerusalem, the one who kill the Prophets and stones those who are sent to her! How often I wanted to gather your children together, as a hen gather her chicks under her wings, and you were not

willing! [25] See! Your house is left to you desolate; [26] for I say to you, you shall see Me no more till you say, "Blessed is He who comes In the Name of the Lord."

7 Take the lowly place

[27] So He told a parable to those who were invited, when He noted how they chose the best places, saying to them: [28] "When you are invited by anyone to a wedding feast, do not sit down in the best place, lest one more honorable than you be invited by him; [29] And he who invited you and him come and say to you; give place to this man; and then you begin with shame to take the lowest place. [30] And when you are invited, go and sit down in the lowest place, so that when he who invited you comes and say to you, "Friend, go up higher", then you will have glory in the presence of those who sit at the table with you. For whoever exalts himself will be humbled, and he who humbles himself will be exalted."

[32] Then He also said to him who invited Him, "When you give a dinner or a supper, do not ask your friends, your brothers, your relatives, nor rich neighbors, lest they also invited you back, and you be repaid. [33] And when you give a feast, invite the poor, the maimed, the lame, the blind. [34] And you will be blessed, because they cannot repay you; for you shall be repaid at the resurrection of the just."

8 The parable of the great supper

[35] Now when one of those who sat at the table with Him heard this thing, he said to Him "Blessed is he who shall eat bread in the Kingdom of God!" [36] Then He said to him "A certain man gave a great supper and invited many, [37] and sent his servant at supper time to say to those who were invited, "Come, for all things are now ready." [38] And they all with one accord began to make excuses. The first say to him, "I have bought a piece of ground, and must go to see it, I ask you to have me excused." [39] One another said, "I have bought five yokes of oxen, and I am going to test them, "So I ask you to have me excused." [40] Still another said, "I have married a wife, and therefore I cannot come.

[41] So that servant came and reported these things to his Master. Then the Master of the house, being angry, said to the servant, "Go out

quickly into the streets and lanes of the city, and bring in here the poor and the maimed and the lame and the blind." And the servant said, "Master it is done as you commanded, and still there is room." [43] Then the Master said to the servant, "Go out into the highways and hedges, and compel them to come in, that my house may be filled. [44] For I say to you that none of those men who were invited shall taste my supper."

9 Leaving all to follow Christ

[45] Now great multitudes went with Him. And He turned and said to them, "Anyone who comes to Me and hate his/her father and mother, spouse and children, brothers and sisters, yes, and his/her life also, he/she cannot be My Disciple. [47] And whoever does not bear his/her cross and come after Me cannot be My Disciple. [48] For which of you, intending to build a tower, does not sit down first and count the cost, whether he/she has enough to finish it--- lest, [49] after he/she has laid the foundation, and is not able to finish, all who see it begin to mock him/her, saying "This man/woman began to build and was not able to finish?

[50] or what King, going to make war against another King, does not sit down first and consider whether he is able with ten thousand to meet him who come against him with twenty thousand? [52] Or else, while the other is still a great way off, he sends a delegation and ask conditions of peace. [53] So likewise, whoever of you do not does not forsake all that he/she has, cannot be My Disciple.

10 The parable of the lost coin

[54] Or what woman, having ten silver coins (called drachma, a valuable coin after worn in a ten- piece garland by married woman), [55] when she loses one coin, does not light a lamp, sweep the house, and search carefully until she finds it? [56] And when she has found it, she called her friends and neighbors together, saying "Rejoice with me, for I have found the piece which I lost." [57] Likewise, I say to you, there is joy in the presence of the Angels of God over one sinner who repents."

CHAPTER 25

<u>1 The parable of the lost son</u>

[1] Then He said: "A certain man had two sons. [2] And the younger of them said to his father; father, give me the portion of goods that falls to me. So, he divided to them his livelihood. [3] and not many days after, the younger son gathered all together, journeyed to a far country, and there waisted his possessions with prodigal living. [4] And when he has spent all, there arose a severe famine in that land, and he began to be in want. [5] then he went to joined himself to a citizen of that country, and he sent him into his fields to feed swine. [6] And he would gladly have filled his stomach with the pods that the swine ate, and no one will give him anything. [7] And when he came to himself, he said, how many of my father's hired servants have bread enough to spare, and I perish with hunger!

[8] I will arise and go to my father, and will say to him, "Father, I have sinned against Heaven and before you, [9] and I am no longer worthy to be called your son. Make me like one of your hired servants." [10] And he arose and came to his father. And when he was still a great way off, his father saw him and had compassion, and ran and fell on his neck and kissed him. [11] And the son said to him, "Father, I have sinned against Heaven and in your sight, and am no longer worthy to be called your son."

[12] And the father said to his servants, "Quickly bring out the best robe and out it on him, and put a ring on his hand and sandals on his feet. [13] And bring the fatted calf here and killed it and let us eat and be merry; [14] for this my son was dead and is alive again; he was lost and is found." And they began to be merry.

¹⁵ Now his older son was in the field. And he came and drew near to the house, he heard music and dancing. ¹⁶ So he called one of the servants and asked what these things meant. ¹⁷ And he said to him, your brother has come, and because he has received him safe and sound, your father has killed the fatted calf. ¹⁸ And he was angry and would not go in. Therefore, his father came out and pleaded with him. ¹⁹ So he answered his father and said to his father, "these many years I have been serving you:

I never transgressed your commandment at any time; and yet you never gave me a young goat, that I might make merry with my friends. ²⁰ And as soon as this son of yours came, who has devoured your livelihood with harlots, you killed the fatted calf for him. ²¹ "And He said to him, "Son, you are always with me, and all that I have is yours. ²² It was right that we should make merry and be glad, for your brother was dead and is alive again, and was lost and is found."

2 The promise of the Holy Spirit

²³ On the last day, that great day of the feast, Jesus stood and cried out, saying, "When anyone thirsts, let him/her come to Me and drink. ²⁴ He/She who believe in Me, as the Scripture has said, out of his/her heart will flow rivers of Living Water." ²⁵ And this is He Who spoke concerning the Spirit, whom those believing in Him would receive; for the Spirit was not yet given, because Jews was not yet glorified.

3 Who is He?

²⁶ therefore, some from the crowd, when they heard this saying, said, "Truly this is the Prophet." ²⁷ Others said, "This is the Christ." And some said, "Will the Christ come out of Galilee? ²⁸ Has not the Scripture said that the Christ come from the seed of David and from the town of Bethlehem, where David was?" ²⁹ So there was a division among the people because of Him. ³⁰ Now some of them wanted to take Him, and no one lay hand on Him.

4 Rejected by authority

³¹ Then the officers came to the Chief-Priests and Pharisees, who said to them, "Why have you not brought Him?" ³² The officers

answered, "No man ever spoke like this Man." ³³ Then the Pharisees answered them, "Are you also deceived? ³⁴ Have any of the rulers or the Pharisees believed In Him? ³⁵ And this crowd that does not know the Law is accursed." ³⁶ Nicodemus (he who came to Jesus by night, being one of them) said, ³⁷ "Does our Law judge a man before it hears him and knows what he is doing?" ³⁸ They answered and said to him, "Are you also from Galilee? Search and look, for no Prophet is to rise out of Galilee."

5 An adulteress faces the Light of the world

³⁹ And everyone went to his own home. And Jesus went to the Mount of Olives. ⁴⁰ Now early, "In the morning He came again in the Temple, and all the people came to Him; and He sat down and Taught them. ⁴¹ Then the Scribes and Pharisees brought to Him a woman caught in adultery. And when they had set her in the midst, ⁴² they say to Him, "Teacher, this woman was caught in adultery, in the very act. ⁴³ Now Moses, in the Law commanded us that such should be stone. And what do you say?" ⁴⁴ This they say, testing Him, that they might have something of which to accuse Him.

And Jesus stooped down and wrote on the ground with His Finger, as though He did not hear. ⁴⁵ So when they continue asking Him, He raised Himself up and said to them, "He who is without sin among you, let him throw a stone at her first." ⁴⁶ And again He stooped down and wrote on the ground. ⁴⁷ Then those who heard it, being convicted by their conscience, went out one by one, beginning with the oldest even to the last. And Jesus was left alone, and the woman standing in the midst. ⁴⁸ When Jesus had raised Himself up and saw no one except the woman, He said to her, "Woman where the accusers of yours? Has no one condemned, you?"

⁴⁹ She said, "No one Lord." And Jesus said to her, "Neither do I condemn you; go and sin no more." ⁵⁰ (later on) And Jesus spoke to them again, saying, "I am the Light of the world. He who follow's Me shall not walk in the darkness, only have the Light of life."

6 Jesus defends His Self-Witness

⁵¹ The Pharisees therefore said to Him, "You bear witness of Yourself; Your witness is not true." ⁵² Jesus answered and said to them,

"Even when I bear witness of Myself, My witness is true, for I know where I came from and where I am going; and you do not know where I come from and where I am going. [53] You judge according to the flesh; I judge no one. [54] And when I do judge, my judgment is True; for I am not alone, I am with the Father Who sent Me.

[55] It is also written in the Law that the testimony of two men is true. [56] I am One who bears witness, and the Father Who sent Me bears witness of Me." [57] Then they said to Him, "Where is Your Father?" Jesus answered, "You know neither Me nor My Father." Supposing you had known Me, you would have known My Father also." [58] These Words that Jesus spoke in the treasury, as He Taught in the Temple; and no one laid hands on Him, for His hour had not yet come.

7 Jesus predicts His departure

[59] Then Jesus said to them again, "I am going away, and you will seek Me, and I will die in your sin. Where I go you cannot come." [60] So the Jews said, "Will kill Himself, because He says, "Where I go you cannot come?" [61] And He said to them, "I am not of this world. [62] There I said to you that you will die in your sins; except you do not believe that I am He, you will die in your sins." [63] then they said to Him, "Who are You." And Jesus said to them, "Just what I have been saying to you from the beginning.

[64] I have many things to say and to judge concerning you, and He Who sent Me is True; and I speak to the world those things which I heard from Him." [65] They did not understand that He spoke to them of the Father. [66] then Jesus said to them, "When you lift up the Son of Man, then you will know that I am He, and that I do nothing of Myself; only as My Father Taught Me, I speak these things. [67] and He Who sent Me is with Me. The Father has not left Me alone, for I always do these things that please Him." [68] As He spoke this Word, many believe in Him.

CHAPTER 26

1 The truth shall make you free

[1] When Jesus said to those Jews who believe Him, "when you abide in My Word, you are My Disciple indeed. [2] And you shall know the truth, and the truth shall make you free." [3] They answered Him, "We are Abraham descendants, and have been in bondage to anyone. How can You say, "You will be made free?" [4] Jesus answered them, "Most assuredly, I say to you, whoever commits sin is a slave of sin. [5] And a slave does not abide in the house forever. [6] Therefore when the Son makes you free, you shall be free indeed.

2 Abraham's seed and Satan

[7] "I know that you are Abraham descendants, and you seek to kill Me, because My Word has no place in you. [8] I speak what I have seen with My Father, and you do what you have seen and heard from My Father." [9] They answered and said to Him, "Abraham is our father." Jesus said to them, "Supposing you were Abraham's children, you would do the work of Abraham. [10] And now you seek to kill Me, a Man who has told you the truth which I heard from God. Abraham did not do this. [11] "You do the deed of your father." Then they said to Him, "We were not born of fornication; we have one Father ---God."

[12] Jesus said to them, "Supposing God was your Father, you would love Me, for I proceeded forth and came from God; nor have I come of Myself, and He sent Me.

Why do you not understand My speech? Because you are not able to listen to My Word. [14] You are of your father the devil, and the desires of your father you want to do. He was a murderer from the beginning, and does not stand in the truth, because there is no truth in him. When he speaks a lie, he speaks from his own resources, for he is a liar and the father of it. [15] And because I tell the truth, you do not believe Me. [16] Which of you convicts Me of sin? And when I tell the truth, why you do not believe Me? [17] He/She who is of God hears God's Words; therefore, you do not hear, because you are not of God."

3 Before Abraham was, I AM

[18] Then the Jews answered and said to Him, "Do we not say rightly that You are a Samaritan and have a demon?" [19] Jesus answered, "I do not have a demon; and I honor My Father, and you dishonor Me. [20] And I do not seek My own glory; there is One who seeks and judges. [21] Most assuredly, I say to you, when anyone keeps My Word, he/she shall never see death." [22] Then the Jews said to Him, "Now we know that you have a demon! Abraham is dead, and the Prophets; and you say, "Anyone who keep My Word he/she shall never taste death."

[23] Are You greater than our father Abraham who is dead? And the Prophets are dead. Who do You make Yourself out to be?" [24] Jesus answered, "When I honor Myself, my honor is nothing. It is My Father Who honor Me, of Whom you say that He is our God.

[25] Yet you have not known Him. And when I say, "I do not know Him, I shall be a liar like you; and I do know Him and keep His Word. [26] Your father Abraham rejoiced to see My day, and He saw it and was glad." [27] Then the Jews said to Him, "You are not yet fifty years old, and you have seen Abraham?" [28] Jesus said to them, "Most assuredly, I say to you. Before Abraham was, I Am." 29 Then the took up stone to throw at Him; and Jesus hid Himself and went out of the Temple.

4 A man born blind receives sight

[30] Now as Jesus passed by, He saw a man who was blind from birth. [31] And His Apostles asked Him, saying," Rabbi, who sinned, this man or his parents, that he was born blind?"

[32] Jesus answered, "Neither this man or his parents sinned, only that the works of God should be revealed in Him. [33] We must work the works of Him Who sent Me while it is day; the night is coming when no one can work. [34] As long that I am in the world, I am the Light of the world." [35] When He Had said this thing, He spat on the ground and made clay with the saliva; and He anointed the eyes of the blind man with the clay.

[36] and He said to him, "Go, wash in the pool of Siloam" (which is translated, --Sent--). And he went and washed, and come back seeing. [37] Therefore the neighbors and those who previously had seen that he was blind said, "Is not this he who sat and begged?" [38] Someone said, "This is he", others said, "He is like him." He said, "I am he." [39] Therefore, they said to him, "How there your eyes opened?" [40] He answered and said, "A Man called Jesus made clay and anointed my eyes and said to me, "Go to Siloam and wash. So, I went and washed, and I received sight." [41] Then they say to him, "Where is He." He said, "I do not know."

5 The Pharisees excommunicate the healed man

[42] They brought him who formerly was blind to the Pharisees. [43] Now it was a Sabbath when Jesus made the clay and opened his eyes. [44] Then the Pharisees also ask him again how he had received his sight. He said to them, "He put clay on my eyes, and I washed, and I see." [45] Therefore some of the Pharisees said, "This Man is not from God, because He does not keep the Sabbath." Others said, "How can a Man who is a sinner do such signs?" And there was a division among them. [46] They said to the (use to be) blind man again, "What do you say about Him because He opened your eyes?" He said He is a Prophet."

[47] And the Jews did not believe concerning him, that he has been blind and received his sight, until they called the parents of him who had received his sight. [48] And they asked them, saying, "Is this your son, who you say was born blind? How does he now see?" His parents

answered them and said, "We know that he is our son, and that he was born blind; [50] and by what means he now see we do not know, or who opened his eyes we do not know.

He is of age; ask him. He will speak for himself." [51] His parents said these things because they feared the Jews, for the Jews have agreed already that when anyone confessed that He was Christ, he/she will be out of the Synagogue. [52] Therefore his parents said, "He is of age ask him." [53] So they again called the man who was blind, and said to him, "Give God the glory! We know that this Man is a sinner."

[54] He answered and said, "Whether He is a sinner or not I do not know. One thing I know: That though I was blind, now I see." [55] Then they said to him again, "What did He do to you? How did He open your eyes?" [56] He answered them, "I told you already, and you did not listen. Why do you want to hear it again? Do you want to become His Disciples?"

[57] Then they reviled him and said, "You are His Disciple, and we are Moses disciples?" [58] We know that God spoke to Moses; as for this fellow, we do not know where He is from." [59] The man answered and said to them, "Why, this is a marvelous thing, that you do not know where He is from: yet He has opened my eyes!

[60] Now we know that God does not hear sinners: and anyone who is a worshiper of God and does His will, He hears him/her. [61] Since the world began it has been unheard of that anyone the eyes of one who was born blind. [62] And this Man was not from God, He could do nothing." [63] And they said to him, "You were completely born in sins, and are you, teachings us?" And they cast him out.

6 True Vision and True blindness

[64] Jesus heard that they had cast him out; and He had found him, He said to him, "Do you believe in the Son of Man?" [65] He answered and said, "Who is He Lord, I may believe in Him?" [66] And Jesus said to him, "You have both see Him and it is He Who is talking with you." [67] Then he said,Lord I believe." And he worshiped Him.

And Jesus said, "For judgment I have come into this world, that those who do not see may see, and that those who see may be blind." [69] Then some of the Pharisees who were with Him heard these Words, and said to Him, "Are we blind also?" [70] Jesus said to them, "Supposing you were blind, you would have no sin; and now you say, "We see" therefore your sins remain."

CHAPTER 27

1 Jesus the True Shepherd

[1] "Most assuredly, I say to you, "He Satan who does not enter the sheepfold by the door, and climb up some other way, the same is a thief and a robber. [2] And he/she Who enters by the door is the Shepherd of the sheep. [3] To him/her the doorkeeper opens, and the sheep hear His voice; and He calls His own sheep, by name and leads them out. [4] And He brings out His own sheep, He goes before them; and the sheep follow Him, for they know His voice.

[5] Yet they will by no means follow a stranger, and will flee from him, for they do not know the voice of strangers." [6] Jesus used this illustration, and they do not understand the things which He spoke to them.

2 Jesus the Good Shepherd

[7] Then Jesus said to them again, "Most assuredly, I say to you, I am the Door of the sheep. [8] All who ever came before Me are thieves and robbers, and the sheep did not hear them. [9] I am the Door. When anyone enters by Me, he/she will be saved, and will go in and out and find pasture [10] the thief does not come except to steal, and to kill, and to destroy. I have come that they may have life, and that they may have it more abundantly. [11] "I am the good Shepherd. The good Shepherd gives His life for His sheep.

[12] And a hireling, he who is not the shepherd, one who does not own the sheep, sees the wolf coming and leaves the sheep and flee; and the wolf catches the sheep and scatters them. [13] The hireling flees because he is a hireling and does not care about the sheep. [14] I am the good Shepherd; and I know My sheep, and I am known by My own. [15]

As the Father know Me, even so I know the Father; and I laid down My life for the sheep. [16] And other sheep I have which are not of this field; them also I must bring, and they will hear My voice; and their will be one flock and one Shepherd.

[17] "Therefore My Father Loves Me, because I lay down My life that I may take it again. [18] No one takes it from Me, and I lay it down Myself. I have Power to lay it down, and I have the Power to take it again. This command that I have received from My Father. [19] Therefore there was a division again among the Jews because of these saying. [20] And many of them said, "He has demon and is mad. Why do you listen to Him?" [21] Others said, "These are not the Words of one who has a demon. Can a demon open the eyes of a blind?"

3 The Shepherd knows His sheep

[22] Now it was the feast of Dedication in Jerusalem, and it was winter. [23] And Jesus walked in the Temple, in Solomon porch. [24] Then the Jews surrounded Him and said to Him, "How long do you keep us in doubt? Knowing You are the Christ, tell us plainly." Jesus answered them, "I told you, and you do not believe. The works that I Do in My Father's Name, they bear witness of Me.

[26] And you do not believe, because you are not My sheep. [27] My sheep hear My voice, and I know them, and they follow Me. [28] And I give them Eternal Life, and they shall never perish; neither shall anyone snatch them out of My hand. [29] My Father, Who has given them to Me, is greater than all; and no one is able to snatch them out of My Father's hand. [30] I and My Father are One."

4 Renewed efforts to stone Jesus

[31] Then the Jews took up stone again to stone Him. [32] Jesus answered them, "Many good works I have shown you from My Father. For which of those works do you stone Me." [33] The Jews answered Him, saying, "For a wood work we do not stone You, except for blasphemy, and because You, being a Man, make Yourself God." [34] Jesus answered them, "Is it not written in your Law, "I said-you are gods-?" [35] So whom He called them gods, to whom the Word of God came. (And the Scripture cannot be broken)

[36] Do you say of Him Whom the Father sanctified and sent into the world, "You are blaspheming" because I said, "I am the Son?" [37] Supposing I do not do the works of My Father, do not believe Me; [38] and when I Do, though you do not believe Me, believe the works, that you may know and understand that the Father is in Me and I in Him." [39] Therefore they sought again to seize Him, except He escaped out of their hand.

5 The believers beyond Jordan

[40] And He went again beyond the Jordan to the place where John was Baptizing at first, and there He stayed. [41] Then many came to Him and said, "John performed no sign, and all the things that John spoke about this Man was True." [42] And many believed in Him there.

6 The death of Lazarus

[43] Now a certain man was sick, Lazarus of Bethany, the town of Mary and her sister Martha. [44] It was that Mary who anointed the Lord with fragrant oil and wiped His feet with her hair, whose brother Lazarus was sick. [45] Therefore the sisters sent to Him, saying "Lord, Behold, he who You love is sick." [46] When Jesus heard that, He said, "This sickness is not into death, except for the glory of God, that the Son of God may be glorified through it."

[47] Now Jesus loved Martha and her sister and Lazarus. (He loved everyone) [48] And, when He heard that he was sick, He stays two more days in the place where He was. [49] Then after this He said to the Apostles, "Let us go to Judea again." [50] The Apostles said to Him, "Rabbi, lately the Jews sought to stone You, and You are going there again?" [51] Jesus answered, "Are they twelve hours in the day? When anyone walk in the day, he/she does not stumble, because he/she the Light of this world. [52] And one walk in the night, he/she stumbles, because the light is not in him/her.

[53] These things He said, and after that He said to them, "Our friend Lazarus sleeps, and I go that I may wake him up." [54] Then His Disciples said, "Lord, well he sleeps he will get well." [55] However, Jesus spoke of His death, and they thought that He was speaking about taking rest in sleep. [56] Then Jesus said to them plainly, "Lazarus is dead. [57] And

I am glad for your sakes that I was not there, that you may believe. Nevertheless, let us go to him." [58] Then Thomas, who is called the twin, said to his fellow Apostles, "Let us go that we may die with him." **(Thomas is a funny, funny man)**

7 I am the Resurrection and the Life

[59] So when Jesus came, He found that he had already been in the tomb for four days. [60] Now Bethany was near Jerusalem, about two miles away. [61] And many of the Jews has joined the women around Martha and Mary, to comfort them concerning their brother. [62] Now Martha, as soon as she heard that Jesus was coming, went and met Him, and Mary was sitting in the house. [63] Now Martha said to Jesus, "Lord it is sad You were not here, my brother would not have die. [64] And even now I know that whatever You ask of God, God will give You."

[65] Jesus said to her, "Your brother will rise again." [66] Martha said to Him, "I know that he will rise in the resurrection at last day." [67] Jesus said to her, "I am the resurrection and the life. Hc/She who believes in Me though he/she may die, he/she shall live. [68] And whoever lives and believes in Me shall never die. Do you believe this?" [69] She said to Him, "Yes, Lord, I believe that You are the Christ, the Son of God, who is to come into the world."

CHAPTER 28

1 Jesus and death, the last enemy

[1] And when she had said these things, she went her way and secretly called Mary her sister, saying, "Teacher as come and He is calling for you." [2] As soon as she heard that, she arose quickly and came to Him. [3] Now Jesus had not yet come into the town, and was at the same place Martha met Him. [4] Then the Jews who were with her in the house, and comforting her, when they saw that Mary rose up quickly and went out, followed her, saying, "She is getting to the tomb and weep there." [5] Then, when Mary came where Jesus was, and saw Him, she fell down at His feet, saying to Him, "Lord, You, had been here, my brother would not have die." [6] Therefore, when Jesus saw her weeping, He groaned in the Spirit and was troubled.[7] And He said, "Where have you laid him?" They say to Him, "Lord, come and see." [8] Jesus wept. [9] Then the Jews said, "See how He loved him!" [10] And some of them said, "Could this Man, who opened the eyes of the blind, also have kept this man from dying?"

2 Lazarus raised from the dead

[11] Then Jesus, again groaning in Himself, came to the tomb. It was a cave, and a stone lay against it. [12] Jesus said, "Take away the stone." Martha, the sister of him who was dead, said to Him, "Lord, by this time there is a stench, for he had been dead four days." [13] Jesus said to her, "Did I say to you that when you believe you will see the glory of God?" [14] Then they took away the stone, and Jesus lifted up His eyes and said, "Father, I Thank You that You have heard Me. [15] And I know that You always hear Me, also because of the people who are standing by, I say this, that they may believe that You sent Me." [16] Now when

He had said these things, He cried with a loud voice, "Lazarus come forth!" [17] And he who had died came out bound hand and foot with graveclothes, and his face was wrapped with a cloth. Jesus said to them, "Loose him, and let him go."

3 The fruitful grain of wheat

[18] Now there were a certain Greeks among those who came up to worship at the feast. [19] Then they came to Philip, who was from Bethsaida of Galilee, and asked him, saying, "Sir, we wish to see Jesus." [20] Philip came and told Andrew, and in turn Andrew and Philip told Jesus. [21] And Jesus answered them, saying, "The hour has come that the Son of Man should be glorified. [22] Most assuredly I say to you, "Unless a grain of wheat falls into the ground and dies, it remains alone, and when it dies, it produces more grain. [23] He/She who loves his/her life will lose it, and he/she who hates his/her life in this world will keep it for Eternal Life. [24] When anyone serves Me, let him/her follow Me; and where I am, there My servant will be also. When anyone serves Me, him/her My Father will honor.

4 Jesus predicts His death on the cross

[25] Now My Soul is troubled, and what shall I say? "Father, save Me from this hour? And the purpose I came to this hour. [26] Father, glorify Your Name." Then a voice came from Heaven, saying, "I have both glorified it and will glorify it again." [27] Therefore the people who stood by and heard it said that it had thundered. Others said, "An Angel has spoken to Him." [28] Jesus answered and said, "This voice did not come because of Me, only for your sake. [29] Now is the judgment of this world; now the ruler of this world will be cast out. [30] And I will be lifted up from the earth, and will draw the people for Myself." [31] This He said, signifying by what death He would die. [32] The people answered Him, "We have heard from the Law that the Christ remains forever; and how can You say, "The Son of Man must be lifted up? Who is this Son of Man?" [33] Then Jesus said to them, "A little while longer the Light is with you. Walk while you have the Light, lest, darkness will overtake you; he/she who walks in darkness does not know where he/she is going. [34] While you have the Light, believe in the Light, that you

become a son and daughter of Light." These things Jesus spoke, and departed, and was hidden from them.

5 Who has believed our report

[35] And although He had done so many signs before them, they did not believe Him, [36] that the word of Isaiah the Prophet might be fulfilled when he spoke:

"Lord who has believed our report? And to whom has the arm of the Lord been revealed" (isaiah53:1)" [37] Therefore they could not believe, because Isaiah said again:

"He has blinded their eyes and hardened their hearts, lest they should see with their eyes, lest they should understand with their heart and turn, so that I should heal them." (isaiah6:10) [38] These things Isaiah said because he saw His glory and spoke of Him.

6 Walk in the Light

[39] Nevertheless even among the rulers many believe in Him, also because of the Pharisees they did not confess Him, lest they should be put out of the Synagogue; [40] for they loved the praise of men more than the praise of God. [41] Then Jesus cried out and said, "He/She who believes in Me, actually believe in Me and also in Him Who sent Me. [42] And he/she who sees Me sees Him Who sent Me. [43] I have come as a Light into the world, that whoever believes in Me should not abide in darkness. [44] And when anyone hears My Words and does not believe, I do not judge him/her; for I did not come to judge the world except to save the world. [45] He/She who rejects Me, and does not receive My Words, has that which judges him/her---The Word that I have spoken will judge you in the last day. [46] For I have not spoken on My own authority; also, the Father Who sent Me gave Me a command, what I should say and what I should speak. [47] And I know that His command is Everlasting Life. Therefore, whatever I speak, just as the Father has told Me, so I speak."

7 Greatness Is Serving

[48] Then James and John, the sons of Zebedee, came to Him, saying, "Teacher, we want You to do for us whatever we ask."[49] And He said

to them, "What do you want Me to do for you "? [50] They say to Him, "Grant us that we may sit, one on Your right hand and the other on your left, in Your glory." [51] And Jesus said to them, "You do not know what you ask. Are you able to drink the cup that I drink, and be Baptize with the Baptism that I am Baptized with": [52] They said to Him, "We are able." And Jesus said to them, "You will indeed drink the cup that I drink, and with, with the Baptism I am Baptized with you will be Baptized; [53] and to sit on My right hand and on My left hand is not Mine to give, it is for those whom it is prepared."

[54] And when the ten heard it, they began to be greatly displeased with James and John. [55] And Jesus called them to Himself and said to them, "You know that those who are considered rulers over the Gentiles lord it over them, and their great one's exercise authority over them. [56] Yet it shall not be so among you; and whoever desires to become great among you shall be your servant. [57] And whoever of you desires to be first shall be slave of all. [58] for even the Son of Man did not come to serve, only to serve, and to give His life a ransom for many."

8 Jesus heals blind Bartimaeus

[59] Now they came to Jericho. As, He went out of Jericho with His Apostles and a great multitude, blind Bartimaeus, the son of Timaeus, sat by the road begging. [60] And when he heard that it was Jesus of Nazareth he began to cry out and say, "Jesus' son of David, have mercy on me!" [61] Then many warned him to be quiet; and he cried out all the more, "Son of David, have mercy on me!" [62] So Jesus stood still and commanded him to be called. Then they called the blind man, saying to him, "Be of good cheer, rise, He is calling you." [63] And throwing aside his garment, he rose and came to Jesus. [64] So Jesus answered and said to him, "What do you want Me to do for you?" The blind man, say to Him, "Rabboni, that I may receive my sight." [65] Then Jesus said to him, "Go your way; your faith has made you well." And immediately he received his sight and followed Jesus on the road.

CHAPTER 29

1 The fig tree withered

[1] Now the next day, when they had come out from Bethany, He was hungry. [2] And seeing from afar a fig tree having leaves, He went to see and perhaps He will find something on it. When He came to it, He found nothing except leaves, for it was not the season for figs. [3] In response Jesus said to it, "Let no one eat fruit from you again." And His Apostles heard it.

2 The lesson of the withered fig tree

[4] Now in the morning, as they passed by, they saw the fig tree dried up from the roots. [5] And Peter, remembering, said to Him, "Rabbi, look! The fig tree which You cursed has withered away." [6] So Jesus answered and said to them, "Have the faith of God." [7] For assuredly, I say to you, whoever says to this mountain, be removed and be cast in the sea; and does not doubt in his/her heart, and believes that those things he/she says, will be done, he/she will have whatever things he/she said. [8] Therefore I say to you, whatever things you ask when you pray, believe that you receive them, and you will have them."

3 Forgiveness in prayer

[9] And whenever you stand praying, and you have something against anyone, forgive him/her, that your Father in Heaven may also forgive you your trespasses. [10] And when you do not forgive him/her, your Father in Heaven will not forgive your own trespasses.

4 Jesus Authority questioned

[11] Now it happened on one of those days, as He taught the people in the Temple and Preached the Gospel, that the Chief Priests and

the Scribes together with the elders confronted Him [12] and spoke to Him, saying, "Tell us, by what authority are You doing these things? Or Who is He Who gave You this authority?" [13] And He answered and said to them, "I also will ask you one thing, and answered Me: The Baptism of John--- was it from Heaven or from men?" [15] And they reasoned among themselves, saying, "Supposing we say, from Heaven, He will say, why did you not believe him? [16] supposing we say, from men, all the people will stone us, for they are persuaded that John was a Prophet." [17] So they answered that they do not know where it was from. [18] And Jesus said to them, "Neither will I tell you by what authority I do these things."

5 Jesus third, time predicts His death and resurrection

[19] Then He took the twelve aside and said to them, "Behold, we are going to Jerusalem, and all things that are written by the Prophets concerning The Son of Man will be accomplished. [20] For He will be delivered to the Gentiles and will be mock and insulted and spit upon. [21] They will scourge Him and kill Him. And the fourth day He will rise again." [22] And they understand none of these things; this saying was hidden from them, and they did not know the things which were spoken.

6 The parable of the wicked vinedressers

[23] Hear another parable: There was a certain landowner who planted a vineyard and set a hedge around it, dug a winepress in it and build a tower. And he leased it to vinedressers and went into a far country. [24] Now when the vintage---time drew near; he sent his servants to the vinedressers, that they might receive its fruit. [25] And the vinedressers took his servants, beat one, killed one, and stone another. [26] Again he sent other servants, more than the first, and they did likewise to them. [27] then last of all he sent his son to them, saying" They will respect my son. [28] And when the vinedressers saw the son, they said among themselves, "This is the heir, come, let us kill him and seize his inheritance.

So, they took him and cast him out of the vineyard and killed him. [30] Therefore, when the owner of the vineyard comes, what will he do to the vinedressers?" 31 They said To Him, "He will destroy those wicked men miserably, and lease his vineyard to other vinedressers who will render to him the fruits of their seasons." 32 Jesus said to them, "Have you never read in the Scriptures: The stone which the builders rejected has become the Chief Cornerstone." (Ps:118.22)

33 Therefore I say to you, "The Kingdom of God will be taken from you and given to a nation bearing the fruits of it. 34 And whoever falls on this stone will be broken; and on whomever it falls, it will grind him to powder." 35 Now when the Chief Priests and Pharisees heard His parable, they perceived that He was speaking of them. 36 And when they sought to lay hands on Him, they feared the multitudes, because they took Him for a Prophet.

7 The Pharisees: Is it lawful to pay taxes to Caesar?

37 So they watched Him, and sent spies who pretend to be righteous, that they might seize on His Words, in order to deliver Him to the power and the authority of the Governor. 38 Then they ask Him, saying, "Teacher, we know that You say and Teach rightly, and You do not show personal favoritism, only Teach the way of God in Truth: 39 Is it lawful for us to pay taxes to Caesar or not?"

And He perceived their craftiness, and said to them, "Why do you test Me? 41 Show Me a denarius. Whose image and inscription doe's it has?" they answered and said, "Caesars."42 And He said to them, "Render therefore to Caesar the things that are Caesar's, and to God the things that are God's." 43 And they could not catch Him in His Words in the presence of the people. And they marveled at His answer and keep silent.

8 The Sadducees: What about the resurrection?

44 Then some of the Sadducees, that deny that there is a resurrection, came to Him and asked Him, 45 saying, "Teacher, Moses wrote to us that when a man's brother dies, having a wife, and he dies without children, his brother should take his wife and raise up offspring for his brother. 46 Now there were seven brothers, and the first took a wife, and died without children. 47 Up to the last brother and none has children.

[48] Last of all the woman died also. [49] Therefore, in the resurrection, whose wife does she become? For all seven had her as wife."

[50] Jesus answered and said to them, "The sons of this age marry and are given in marriage. [51] And those who are counted worthy to attain this age, and the resurrection of the dead, neither marry nor are given in marriage; [52] Nor can they die anymore, for they are equal to the Angels and are sons of God, being sons of the resurrection.

[53] And even Moses showed in the "burning bush passage" that the dead are raised, when he called the Lord—The God of Abraham, the God of Isaac, and the God of Jacob. (Exodus3:6). [54] For He is not the God of the dead only of the living, for all live to Him." [55] Then some of the Scribes answered and said, "Teacher You have spoken well."[56] And after that they dared not question anymore.

9 The Scribes: Which is the first commandment of all?

[57] Some of the Scribes came, and having heard them reasoning together, perceiving that He had answered them well, asked Him, "Which is the first commandment of all?" [58] Jesus answered him, "The first of all commandment is: Hear O Israel, the Lord our God, The Lord is One?" [59] "And you shall love the Lord your God with all your heart, with all your soul, with all your mind, and with all your strength." (Deuteronomy 6: 4-5) [60] And the second, like it, is this: "You shall love your neighbor as yourself:(Leviticus19:18) There is no other commandment greater than these."

[61] So the Scribes said to Him, "Well said, Teacher. You have spoken the Truth, for there is one God, and there is no other except He. [62] And to love Him with all your heart, with all the understanding, and with all the strength, and to love one's neighbor as oneself, is more than all the burn offerings and sacrifices." [63] Now when Jesus saw that he answered wisely, He said to him, "You are not far from the Kingdom of God." And after that no one dared question Him.

10 Jesus: How can David call his descendants Lord?

[64] While the Pharisees were gathered together, Jesus asked them, [65] saying, "What do you think about the Christ? whose Son is He?" They

said to Him, "the son of David." [66] He said to them, "How then does David in the Spirit call Him, "Lord" saying: [67] "The Lord said to my Lord, sit at My right hand, till I make Your Enemies Your footstool?"

(Ps:110,1) [68] So David then called Him Lord---How is He then his Son?" [69] And no one was able to answer Him a word, nor from that day on did anyone dare question Him anymore. **This is the third time that we saw the same statement, that is: And no one dared to question Him anymore. I don't think that Luke wrote this. When Luke was writing his Gospel, he knew that they will always be other question by the Scribes and Pharisees. And he will not have made that statement. It was added probably later to make him not trustworthy. And to say that these pharisees dare, no I believe that evil people will not relinquish their efforts to make you fall. I believe that statement was added when they put the whole Bible together. It was bad theologians and bad scholars who put that statement there. (I despise their action and they really make me mad)**

11 Beware of the Scribes

[70] Then, in the hearing of all the people, He said to His Apostles, [71] "Beware of the Scribes, who desire to go around in long robes, love greetings in the marketplaces, the best seats in Synagogues, and the best places at feasts. [72] Who devour widow's houses, and for a pretense make long prayers. They will receive greater condemnation."

CHAPTER 30

1 The widow's two mites

[1] Now Jesus sat opposite the treasury and saw how the people put money into the treasury. And many who were rich put in much. [2] Then one widow came and threw in two mites. So, He called His Apostles to Himself and said to them, "Assuredly, I say to you that this poor widow has put in more than all those who have given to the treasury; [3] for they all put in out of their abundance. Except she, out of her poverty put in all that she had, her whole livelihood."

2 Jesus predicts the destruction of the Temple

[4] Then, as spoke of the Temple, how it was adorned with beautiful stones and donations, He said, [5] "These things which you see---the days will come in which not one stone shall be left upon another that shall not be thrown down."

3 The signs of the times and the end of the age

[6] Now as He sat on the Mount of Olives opposite the Temple, Peter, James, John and Andrew asked Him privately, "Teacher, and when these things be? And what sign will there be when these things are about to take place?" [7] And He said: "Take heed that you not be deceived. For many will come in My Name, saying, I am He, and the time has draw near, do not go after them. [8] And you hear of wars and commotions, do not be terrified; for these things must come to pass first, and the end will not come immediately." [9] Then He said to them, "Nation will rise against nation, and Kingdom against Kingdom. [10] And there will be great earthquakes in various places, and famines and pestilences; and they will be fearful sights and great signs from Heaven.

[11] And before all these things, they will lay their hands on you and persecute you, delivering you up to the Synagogues and prisons. You will be brought before Kings and rulers for My Name's sake. [12] And I will turn out for you as an occasion for testimony. [13] Therefore settle it in your heart not to meditate beforehand on what you will answer.

[14] For I will give you a mouth and wisdom which all your adversaries will not be able to contradicts or resist. [15] You will be betrayed even by parents and brothers, relatives and friends; and they put some of you to death. [16] And you will be hated by all for My Name's sake. [17] And he/she who endures to the end shall be saved."

4 The great tribulation

[18] "So when you see the Abomination of desolation" (Daniel 11:31---12:11) spoken by Daniel the Prophet, standing where it ought not, "then let those who are in Judea flee to the mountains. [19] Let him/her who is on housetops not go down into the house, nor enter to take anything out of the house. [20] And let him/her who is in the field not go back to get his/her clothes. [21] And woe to those who are pregnant, and to those who are nursing babies in these days! [22] And pray that your flight may not be in winter. [23] For in those days there will be tribulation, such as has not seen since the beginning of the creation which God created until this time, nor ever shall be.

[24] And unless the Lord had shortened those days, no flesh will be saved; except for the elect's sake, whom He chose, He shortened the days. [25] Then when anyone says to you, "Look, here is Christ!" or, "Look, He is there!" do not believe it. [26] For false Christ and false prophets will rise and show signs and wonders to deceive, even the elect. [27] And to heed; see, I have told you all things beforehand."

5 The coming of the Son of Man

[28] Immediately after the tribulation of those days the sun will be darkened, and the moon will not give its light; the stars will fall from Heaven, and the Powers of the Heavens will be shaken. [29] Then the sign of the Son of Man will appear in Heaven, and then all the tribes of the earth will mourn, and they will see the Son of Man coming on the clouds of Heaven with Power and great glory. [30] And He will sent His

Angels with a great sound of a trumpet, and they will gather together His elects from the four winds, from one end of the Heaven to the other.

6 The parable of the fig tree

[31] Now learn this parable from the fig tree: When its branch has already become tender and puts forth leaves, you know that summer is near. [32] So you also, when you see all these things, know that it is near---at the doors! [33] Assuredly, I say to you, "This generation will by no means pass away till all these things take place. [34] Heaven and earth will pass away, and My Words by no means pass away."

7 No one knows the day or hour

[35] And of that day and hour no one knows, not even the Angels of Heaven, except My Father Only. [36] And as the days of Noah were, so also will the coming of the Son of Man be. [37] For as in the days before the flood, they were eating and drinking, marrying and giving in marriage, until the day that Noah entered the ark, [38] and did not know until the flood came and took them all away, so also with the coming of the Son of Man be.

[39] Then two men will be in the field: one will be taken and the other one left. [40] Two women will be grinding at the mill: one will be taken and the other one left. [41] Watch therefore, for you do not know what day your Lord is coming. [42] And know this, when the Master of the house had known what day/hour the thief will come, he would have watched and not allowed his house to be broken into. [43] And know this, a man/woman going to a far country, who left his/her house and gave authority to his/her servants, and to each his/her work, and commanded the doorkeepers to watch.

[44] Watch therefore, for you do not know when the Master of the house is coming—in the evening, at midnight, at the crowing of the roaster, or in the morning, lest, [45] coming suddenly, he found you sleeping. [46] And what I say to you, I say to all: Watch!"

8 The parable of the two sons

[47] A man had two sons, and he came to the first and said, "Son, go, work today in my vineyard." [48] He answered and said, "I will not." And

afterward he regretted and went. [49] Then he came to the second and said likewise. And he answered and said, "I go, Sir and he did not go. [50] Which of the two did the will of the father?" they said to him, "The first." Jesus said to them, "Assuredly, I say to you that tax collectors and harlots enter the Kingdom before you. [51] For John came to you in the way of righteousness, and you did not believe him; and tax collectors and harlots believed him, and when you saw it, you did not afterward relent and believe him.

9 The parable of the wedding feast

[52] And Jesus spoke to them again in parables and said: [53] "The Kingdom of Heaven is like a certain King who arranged a marriage for his son, [54] and sent out his servants to call those who were invited to the wedding; and they were not willing to come. [55] Again, he sent out others servants, saying, "Tell those who were invited, see, I have prepared my dinner; my oxen and fatten cattle are killed, and the things are ready. Comme to the wedding." [56] And they made light of it and went their ways, one to his own farm, another to his business. [57] And the rest seizes his servants, treated them spitefully, and killed them.

[58] And when the King heard about it, he was furious. And he sent out his armies, destroyed those murderers, and burned their city. [59] Then he said to his servants, the wedding is ready, and those who were invited were not worthy. [60] Therefore go into the highways, and as many as you find, invite to the wedding: [61] so those servants went out into the highways and gathered together all whom they found, both bad and good. And the wedding hall was filled with guests.

[62] And the King came in to see the guests, he saw a man there who did not have a wedding garment. [63] So he said to him, "Friend, how did you come in here without a wedding garment? And he was speechless. [64] Then the King said to the servants, bind him hand and foot, and cast him in outer darkness; there will be weeping and gnashing of teeth." "For many are called, and few are chosen."

CHAPTER 31

<u>1 The parable of the workers in the vineyard</u>

¹ "For The Kingdom of Heaven is like a landowner who went out early in the morning to hire laborers for his vineyard." ² Now when he had agreed with laborers for a denarius a day, he sent them into the vineyard. ³ And he went about the third hour and saw other standing idle in the marketplace, ⁴ and said to them, "You also go into the vineyard, and whatever is right I will give you; and they went. ⁵ Again he went out about the six and the ninth hour, and did likewise. ⁶ And about the eleven he went out and found others standing, and said to them, "Why have you been standing here idle all day?" ⁷ They said to him, "Because no one hired us." He said to them, "You also, go into the vineyard, and whatever is right you will receive."

⁸ So when evening had come, the owner of the vineyard said to his steward, "Call the laborers and give them their wages, beginning with the last to the first." ⁹ And when those who came were hired about the eleven hour, they each received a denarius. ¹⁰ And when the first came, they supposed that they would receive more and they likewise received a denarius. ¹¹ And when they had received it, they complained against the landowner, ¹² saying, "There last men have worked only one hour, and you made them equal to us who have borne the burden and the heat of the day." ¹³ And he answered one of them and said, "Friend, I am doing you no wrong. Did you not agree with me for a denarius? Take what is yours and go your way. I wish to give to the last man the same as to you. ¹⁵ Is it not lawful for me to do what I wish with my own things? Or is your eye evil because I am good." ¹⁶ So the last will be first, and the first last.

2 Two blind men receive their sight

[17] Now as they went out of Jericho, a great multitude followed Him. [18] And Behold, two blind men sitting by the road, when they heard that Jesus was passing by, cried out, saying, "Have mercy on us, O Lord, Son of David." [19] Then the multitude warned them that they should be quiet; and they cried out the more, saying, "Have mercy on us, O Lord, Son of David." [20] So Jesus stood still and called them, and said, "what do you want Me to do for you." [21] They say to Him, "Lord, that our eyes may be opened." [22] So Jesus had compassion and touched their eyes. And immediately their eyes received sight, and they follow Him.

3 Woe to the Scribes and Pharisees

[23] Then Jesus spoke to the multitudes and to His Apostles, [24] saying, "The Scribes and the Pharisees sit in Moses' seat. [25] Therefore whatever they tell you, to observe and do, only observe and do not according to their works; for they say, and do not. [26] For they bind heavy burdens, hard to bears, and lay them on men shoulders; and they themselves will not move them with one of their fingers. [27] And all their works they do is to be seen by men. They make their phylacteries broad and enlarge the borders of their garments. [28] They love the best places at feast, the best seat in the Synagogues, [29] greetings in marketplaces, and to be call by men, "Rabbi, Rabbi." [30] And you do not be call Rabbi; for One is your Teacher and you are all brethren. [31] Do not call anyone on earth your father; for One is your Father, He Who is in Heaven. [32] And do not be called teachers; for One is your Teacher, the Christ. [33] And he who is greatest among you shall be your servant. [34] And whoever exalts himself will be humbled, and he who humbles himself will be exalted.

[35] And woe to you, Scribes and Pharisees, hypocrites! For you shut up the Kingdom of Heaven against men; for you neither go yourselves, nor do you allow those who are entering to go in. [36] Woe to you, Scribes and Pharisees, hypocrites! For you devours widow's houses, and for a pretense make long prayers. Therefore, you will receive greater condemnation. [37] Woe to you, Scribes and Pharisees, hypocrites! For travel land and sea to win one proselyte, and when he is won, you make him twice as much a son of hell as yourselves.

[38] Woe to you, blind guides who say, "Whoever who swears by the Temple, it is nothing; and whoever swears by the gold of the Temple, he is obliged to perform it.[39] Fools and blind! For which is greater, the gold or the Temple that sanctified the gold? [40] And, whoever swears by the Altar, it is nothing; and whoever swears by the gift that is on it, he is obligated to perform it. [41] Fools and blind! For which is greater, the gift or the Altar that sanctified the gift? [42] Therefore he who swear by the Altar, swear by it and by all things on it. [43] He who swears by the Temple, swears by it and by Him who dwelt in it. [44] And he who swears by the Heaven, swears by the throne of God and by Him Who sits on it.

[45] Woe to you, Scribes and Pharisees, hypocrites! For you pay tithe of mint and anise and cumin, and have neglected the weightier matters of the Law; Justice and Mercy and Faith. These you ought to have done, without leaving the others undone. [46] Blind guides, who strain out a gnat and swallow a camel! [47] Woe to you, Scribes and Pharisees, hypocrites! For you cleanse the outside of the cup, and dish, and inside they are full of extortion and self-indulgence.

[48] Blind Pharisees, first cleanse the inside of the cup and dish, that the outside of them maybe clean also.[49] Woe to you, Scribes and Pharisees, hypocrites! For you are like whitewashed tombs which indeed appear beautiful outwardly, and inside are full of dead men's bones and all uncleanness. [50] Even so you also outwardly appear righteous to men, except inside you are full of hypocrisy and lawlessness. [51] Woe to you, Scribes and Pharisees, hypocrites! Because you build the tombs of the Prophets and adorn the monuments of the righteous, [52] and say, "Only we had lived in the days of our fathers, we would not have been partakers with them in the blood of the Prophets."

[54] Therefore you are witnesses against yourselves that you are sons of those who murdered the Prophets. [55] Fill up, then, the measure of your father's guilt. [56] Serpents, brood of vipers! How can you escape the condemnation of hell? [57] Therefore indeed, I send Prophets, wise men, and Scribes: some of them you will kill and crucify, and some of them you will scourge in your Synagogues and persecute from city to city, [58] that on you may come all the righteousness blood shed on the earth, from the blood of righteous Abel to the blood of Zechariah, son of

Berechiah, whom you murdered between the Temple and the Altar, [59] Assuredly, I say to you, all these things will come upon this generation.

4 The parable of the wise and foolish virgins

[60] Then the Kingdom of Heaven shall be likened to ten virgins who took their lamps and went out to meet the bridegroom. [61] Now five of them were wise, and five of them foolish. [62] Those who were foolish took their lamps and took no oil with them, [63] and the wise took oil in their vessels with their lamps. [64] And while the bridegroom was delayed, they all slumbered and slept.

[65] And at midnight a cry was heard: Behold, the Bridegroom, lets go out to meet Him! [66] Then all those virgins arose and trimmed their lamps. [67] And the foolish said to the wise, "Give us some of your oil, for our lamps are going out."

[68] And the wise answered, saying, "No, lest there should not be enough for us and you; you can go rather to those who sell, and buy for yourselves." [69] And while they went to buy, the bridegroom came, and those who were ready went in with Him to the wedding; and the door was shut. [70] Afterward the others virgins came also, saying, "Lord, Lord, open to us!" [71] And he answered and said, "Assuredly, I say to you, I do not know you." [72] Watch therefore, for you know neither the day nor the hour.

5 The Law, the Prophets and the Kingdom

[73] Now the Pharisees, who were lovers of money, also heard all these things, and they derided Him. [74] And He said to them, "You are those who justify yourselves before men, and God know your hearts. For what is highly esteemed among men, is an abomination in the sight of God. [75] The Law and the Prophets were until John. Since that time the Kingdom of God has been preached, and everyone is pressing into it."

CHAPTER 32

<u>1 The parable of the talents</u>

[1] For the Kingdom of Heaven is like a man traveling to a far country, who called his own servants and delivered his good to them. [2] And to one he gave five talents, to another two, and to another one to each according to his own ability; and immediately he went on a journey. [3] Then he/she who had receive five talents went and trade with them, and made another five talents. [4] And likewise he/she who had received two gained two more also. [5] And he/she who had receive one went and dug a hole in the ground, and hid his lord's money. [6] After a long time the lord of those servants came and settle accounts with them. [7] So he/she who had receive five talents came and brought five more talents besides them."

"Lord, you delivered to me five talents, look, I have gained five more talents besides them." [8] His lord said to him/her, "Well done, good and faithful servant; you were faithful over a few things, I will make you ruler over many things, enter into the joy of your lord." [9] He/She also who had received two talents come and said, "Lord, you delivered two me two talents; look, I have gain two more talents besides them."

[10] His lord said to him/her, "Well done, good and faithful servant; you have been faithful over a few things, I will make ruler over many things, enter into the joy of your lord." [11] then he/she who had receive one talent came and said, "Lord, I knew you to be a hard man, reaping where you have not sow, and gathering where you have not scattered seed. [12] And I was afraid, and went and hid your talent in the ground." Look, there you have what is yours: [13] And his/her lord answered and said to him/her, "You wicked and lazy servant, you knew that I reap where I have not sown, and gather where I have not scattered seed.

¹⁴ So you ought to have deposited my money with the bankers, and at my coming I would have received back my own with interest. ¹⁵ So take the talent from him/her, and give it to him/her who has ten talents. ¹⁶ For to everyone who has, more will be given, and he/she will have abundance; and from him/her who does not have, even what he/she has will be taken away. ¹⁷And cast the unprofitable servant into the outer darkness. There will be weeping and gnashing of teeth."

2 The Son of Man will judge the nations

¹⁸ "When the Son of Man comes in His glory, and all the Angels with Him, then He will sit on the throne of His glory. ¹⁹ All the nations will be gathered before Him, and He will separate them one from another, as a shepherd divides his sheep from the goats. ²⁰ And He will set the sheep on his right hand, and the goats on the left. ²¹ Then the King will say to those on His right hand, "Come, you blessed of My Father, inherit the Kingdom prepared for you from the foundation of the world." ²² "For I was hungry and you gave Me food; I was thirsty and you give Me drink; I was a stranger and you took Me in; ²³ I was naked and you, cloth Me; I was sick and you visited Me; I was in prison and you came to Me."

²⁴ Then the righteous will answer Him, saying, "Lord, when did we see You hungry and feed You, or thirsty and give You drink? ²⁵ When did we see You as stranger, and take You in, or naked and clothe You? ²⁶ Or when did we see You sick, or in prison, and come to You?" ²⁷ And the King will answer and say to them, "Assuredly, I say to you, in as much as you did it to one of the least of these My brethren, you did it to Me."

²⁸ Then He will also say to those on the left hand," Depart from Me, you cursed, into the everlasting fire prepared for the devil and his angels" ²⁹ for I was hungry and you gave Me no food; I was thirsty and you gave Me no drink; ³⁰ I was a stranger and you did not take Me in, naked and you did not clothe Me, sick and in prison and you not visit Me. ³¹ Then they will answer, saying, "Lord, when did we see You hungry or thirsty or a stranger or naked or sick or in prison and did not ministered to You?" ³² Then He will answer them, saying," Assuredly, I say to you, inasmuch you did not do it to one of the least of these,

you did not do it to Me." ³³ And these will go away into everlasting punishment, and the righteous into Eternal Life.

3 The parable of the unjust steward

³⁴ He also said to His Apostles: "There were a certain rich man who had a steward, and an accusation was brought to him that this man was wasting good. ³⁵ So he called him and said to him, "What is this I hear about you? give an account of your stewardship, for you can no longer be steward." ³⁶ Then the steward said within himself, "What shall I do? For my master is taking the stewardship away from me. I cannot dig; I am ashamed to beg. ³⁷ I have resolved what to do, that when I am put out of the stewardship, they may receive me into their house." ³⁸ So he called everyone of his Master's debtors to him, and said to the first, how much do you owe my Master? ³⁹ And he said, a hundred measure of oil, he said to him, take your bill, and sit down quickly and write fifty."

⁴⁰ Then he said to another, and how much that you owe? And he said, a hundred measures of wheat, and he said to him, take your bill and write eighty. ⁴¹ So the Master commended the unjust steward because he had delt shrewdly. For the sons of this world are shrewder in their generation than the son of Light.⁴² And I say to you, make friends for yourselves by unrighteous mammon, that when it fails, they may receive you into an everlasting home. ⁴³ He who is faithful in what is least is faithful also in much; and he who is unjust in what is least is unjust also in much;⁴⁴ Therefore when you have not been faithful in the unrighteousness mammon, who will commit to your trust the true riches?

⁴⁵ And when you have not been faithful in what is another man's, who will give you what is your own? ⁴⁶ No servants can serve two masters; for either he will the one and love the other, or else he will be loyal to the one and despise the other. You cannot serve God and mammon.

CHAPTER 33

1 Faith and duty

¹ And the Apostles said to the Lord, "Increase our faith." ² So the Lord said, "Supposing you have faith as a mustard seed, you can say to this mulberry tree, "Be pulled up by the roots and be planted in the sea; and it would obey you. ³ And which of you, having a servant plowing or tending sheep, will say to him when he has come in the front of the field, come at one and sit down to eat?" ⁴ Instead will he not rather say to him, prepare something for my supper, and gird yourself and serve me till I have eaten and drunk, and afterward you will eat and drink?" ⁵ Does he thank that servant because he did the things that were commanded him? I think not. ⁶ So likewise you, when you have done all those things which you are commanded, say, "We are unprofitable servants. We have done what was our duty to do."

2 The lepers cleansed

⁷ Now it happened as He went to Jerusalem that He passed through the midst of Samaria and Galilee. ⁸ Then as He entered a certain village, there met Him ten men who were lepers, who stood afar off. ⁹ And they lifted up their voices and said, "Jesus, Master, have mercy on us!" ¹⁰ When he saw them, He said to them, "Go show yourselves to the Priests." And so it was that as they went, they were cleansed. ¹¹ And one of them, when he saw that he was healed, returned, and with a loud voice glorified God.¹² And fell down on his face at His feet, giving Him thanks. And he was a Samaritan. ¹³ So Jesus answered and said, "Were not ten cleansed? And where are the nine? ¹⁴ Where there not any found who returned to give glory to God except this foreigner?"

¹⁵ And He said to him, "Arise, go your way. Your faith has made you well."

3 The parable of the persistent widow

¹⁶ Then He spoke a parable to them, that men always ought to pray and not lose heart, ¹⁷ saying, "There was in a certain city a judge who did not fear God nor regard man." ¹⁸ Now there was a widow in that city; and she came to him, saying, "Get justice from me from my adversary." ¹⁹ And he would not for a while; and afterward he said within himself, "Though I do not fear God nor regard man, ²⁰ yet because this widow troubles me I will avenge her, lest by her continual coming she weary me."

²¹ Then the Lord said," Hear what the unjust judges said. ²² And shall God not avenge His own elects who cry out day and night to Him though He bears long with them? ²³ I tell you that He will avenge speedily. Nevertheless, when the Son of Man comes, will He find faith on the earth?"

4 The parable of the Pharisee and the tax collector

²⁴ Also He spoke this parable to some who trusted in themselves that they were righteous, and despised others: ²⁵ Two men went up to the Temple to pray, one a Pharisee and the other a tax collector. ²⁶ The Pharisee stood and prayed thus with himself, "God, I Thank You that I am not like other men---extortioner, unjust, adulterers, or even as his tax collector. ²⁷ I fast twice a week; I give tithes of all that I posses." ²⁸ And the tax collector, standing afar off, will not so much as raise his eyes to Heaven, and beat his breast, saying, "God, be merciful to me a sinner." ²⁹ I tell you; this man went to his house justified rather than the other; for everyone who exalt himself/herself will be humbled, and he/she who humbles himself/herself will be exalted."

5 Jesus comes to Zacchaeus' house

³⁰ Then Jesus entered and passed through Jericho. ³¹ Now Behold, there was a man named Zacchaeus who was a chief tax collector, and he was rich. ³² And he sought to see Who Jesus was, and could not because of the crowd, for he was a short stature. ³³ So he ran ahead and

climb up into a sycamore tree to see Him, for He was going to pass that way. ³⁴ And when Jesus camo to the place, He looked up, and said to him, "Zacchaeus, make haste and come down, for today I must stay at your house." ³⁵ So he made haste and came down, and received Him joyfully. ³⁶ And when they saw it, they all complained, saying, "He has gone to be a guest with a man who is a sinner."

³⁷ Then Zacchaeus stood and said to the Lord, "Look Lord, I give half of my good to the poor; and when I have taken anything from anyone by false accusation, I restore fourfold." ³⁸ And Jesus said to him, "Today salvation has come to this house, because he also is a son of Abraham; ³⁹ for the Son of Man has come to seek and to save that which was lost."

6 The parable of the minas

⁴⁰ Now as they heard these things, He speak another parable, because He was near Jerusalem and because they thought the Kingdom of God will appear immediately. ⁴¹ Therefore, He said: "A nobleman when to a far country to receive for himself a kingdom and to return." ⁴² So he called ten of his servants, delivered them ten minas, and said to them, "Do business till I come." ⁴³ And his citizens hated him, and sent a delegation after him, saying, "We will not have this man reign over us."

⁴⁴ And so it was when he returned, having received the kingdom, he then commanded the servants, to whom he had given them the money, to be called to him, that he might know how much every man had gained by trading. ⁴⁵ Then came the first, saying, "Master, your minas have earned ten minas." ⁴⁶ And he said to him/her, "Well done good servant; because you were faithful in a very little, have authority over ten cities." ⁴⁷ And the second came, saying, "Master, your minas had earned five minas." ⁴⁸ Likewise he said to him/her, "You also be over five cities."

⁴⁹ Then another came, saying, "Master, here is your mina, which I have kept put away in a handkerchief. ⁵⁰ For I fear you, because you are an austere man. You collect what you did not deposit, and reap what you did not sow." ⁵¹ And he said to him/her, "Out of your mouth I will

judge you, you wicked servant. You knew that I was an austere man, collecting what I did not deposit and reaping what I did not sow.

[52] Why then did you not put the money in the bank, that I my coming I might have collected it with interest?" [53] And he said to those who stood by, "Take the mina from him/her, and give it to him/her who has ten minas." [54] "For I say to you, that to everyone who has will be given; and for him/her who does not have, even what he/she has will be taken away from him/her. [55] And bring here the enemies of mine, who did not want me to reign over them, and slay them before me."

7 The coming of the Kingdom

[56] Now when He was asked by the Pharisees when the Kingdom of God will come, He answered them and said, "The Kingdom of God do not come with observation; [57] nor will they say, --see here or see there—for indeed, the Kingdom of God is within you." [58] Then He said to the Disciples, "The days will come when you will desire to see one of the days of the Son of Man, and you will not see it. [59] And they will say to you, "Look here!" Do not go after them or follow them. [60] For as the lightning that flashes out of one part under Heaven shines to the other part under Heaven, so also the Son of Man will be in His day. [61] Only He must suffer many things and be rejected by this generation."

[62] And at it was in the days of Noah, so it will be also in the days of the Son of Man: [63] They ate, they drank, they married wives, they were given in marriage, until the day that Noah entered the Ark, and the flood came and destroyed them all. [64] Likewise as it was also in the days of Lot: they ate, they drank, they bought, they sold, they planted, they build; [65] and on that day that Lot went out of Sodom it rained fire and brimstone from Heaven and destroyed them all. [66] Even so will it be in the day when the Son of Man is revealed. [67] In that day, he/she who is on the housetop, and his/her good are in the house, let him/her come down to take them away. And likewise, the one who is in the field, let him/her not turn back.

[68] Remember Lot's wife. [69] Whoever seeks to save his/her life will lose it, and whoever loses his/her life will perverse it. [70] I tell you, in that night they will be two men in one bed: the one will be taken and the other will be left. [71] Two women will be grinding together: the one

will be taken and the other left. ⁷² two men will be in the field: the one will be taken and the other left."

⁷³ And they answered and said to Him, "Where, Lord?" And, He said to them, "Wherever the body is, there the eagles will be gathered together"

CHAPTER 34

1 The plot to kill Jesus

¹ Now it came to pass, when Jesus had finished all these saying, that He said to His Apostles, ² "You know that after two days is the Passover, and the Son of Man will be delivered up to be crucified." ³ Some of the Jews did believe in Him, and others decided to go to the Pharisees and tell them what He did. ⁴ The Chief Priests Caiaphas, gathered a council and said, "What shall we do? For this Man works many signs. ⁵ And we let Him alone like this, everyone will believe in Him, and the Romans will come and take away both our place and nation." ⁶ Caiaphas said, "Do you consider that it is expedient for us that one Man should die for the people, and not that the whole nation should perish." ⁷ Now this He did not say on His own authority; and being High Priest (Caiaphas) that year he prophesied that Jesus would die for the nation, ⁸ and not for the nation only, that also He would gather together in one of the children of God who were scattered abroad.

⁹ From that day on, they plotted to put Him to death. ¹⁰ Therefore Jesus no longer walked openly among the Jews, and went from there into the country near the wilderness, to a city called Ephraim, and there remained with His Apostles. ¹¹ And the Passover of the Jews was near, and many went from the country up to Jerusalem before the Passover, to purify themselves.

¹² Then Satan entered Judas, surnamed Iscariot, who was numbered among the twelve. ¹³ So he went his way and conferred with the Chief Priests and captains, how he might betray Him to them. And they were glad, and agreed to give him money. ¹⁴ So he promised and sought opportunity to betray Him to them in the absence of the multitude.¹⁵ Not during the feast, lest there be an uproar among the people.

2 The anointing at Bethany

[16] And when Jesus was in Bethany at the house of Martha, the sister of Lazarus. [17] There they make Him a supper; and Martha served, and Lazarus was one of those who sat at the table with Him. [18] Then Mary took a pound of a very costly oil of spikenard, anointed the feet of Jesus, and wiped His feet with her hair. And the house was filled with the fragrance of the oil. [19] And one of the Apostles Judas Iscariot said, "Why was the fragrant oil not sold for three hundred denarii and given to the poor?" This he said, not he cared for the poor, except because he was a thief, and had the money box; and he used to take what was put in it. [20] And Jesus said, "Let her alone; she has kept this for the day of My burial. [21] For the poor you have with you always, and Me you do not have always."

3 The plot to kill Lazarus

[22] Now a great many of the Jews knew that He was there; and they came, not for Jesus sake's only, instead that they might also see Lazarus, whom He had raised from the dead. [23] And the Chief Priests plotted to put Lazarus to death also, [24] because on account of him, many of the Jews went away and believed in Jesus.

4 The triumphal entry

[25] Now when they drew near Jerusalem, and came to Bethphage, at Mount of Olives, then Jesus sent two Apostles, [26] saying to them, "Go in the village opposite you, and immediately you will find a donkey tied, and a colt with her. Loose them and bring them to Me. [27] And that anyone says anything to you, you shall say, "The Lord has need of them", and immediately he will send them." [28] This was done that it might be fulfilled which was spoken by the Prophet, saying, [29] "Tell the daughter of Zion, Behold, your King is coming to you, lowly, and sitting on a donkey, a colt, a foal of the donkey."

[30] So the Apostles went and did as Jesus commanded them. [31] They brought the donkey and the colt, laid their clothes on them, and sat Him on the colt. [32] And a great multitude spread their clothes on the road. [33] Then the multitude who went before and those who followed cried out saying: "Hosanna to the Son of David! Blessed is He who

comes in the Name of the Lord! Hosanna in the Highest!" [34] And when He had come into Jerusalem, all the city was moved, saying, "Who is this?" [35] And the multitude said, "This is Jesus, the Prophet from Nazareth of Galilee."

5 Jesus washes the Apostles feet

[36] Now before the feast of the Passover, when Jesus knew that His hour had come that He should depart from this world to the Father, having loved His own who were in the world, He loved them to the end. [37] And supper being ended, the devil having already put it into the heart of Judas Iscariot, Simon's son, to betray Him, [38] Jesus, knowing the Father had given all things into His hands, and that He had come from God and was going to God, [39] rose from supper and laid aside His garments, took a towel and girded Himself. [40] After that, He poured water in a basin and began to wash the Apostle's feet, and to wipe them with the towel with which He was girded.

[41] Then He came to Simon Peter. And Peter said to Him, "Lord, are You washing my feet?" [42] Jesus answered and said to him, "What I am doing you do not understand now, you will know after this." [43] Peter said to Him, "You shall never wash my feet." Jesus answered him, "I have to do it, or you have no part of Me." [44] Simon Peter said to Him" Lord, not my feet only, also my hands and my head."[45]Jesus said to him, "He who is bathed needs only to wash his feet, and he is completely clean, and you are clean, except not all of you."

[46] For He knew who would betray Him; therefore, He said, "You are not all clean." [47] So when He had washed their feet, taken His garments, and sat down again, He said to them, "Do you know what I have done to you? [48] You call Me Teacher and Lord, and you say well, for so I am. [49] So, I then, your Lord and Teacher, have washed your feet, you also ought to wash one another feet. [50] For I have given you an example, that you should do as I done to you.

[51] Most assuredly, I say to you, a servant is not greater than his/her Master, nor is He Who is sent greater than He Who sent Him. [52] When you know these things, blessed are you when you do them?"

6 Jesus identifies His betrayer

[53] "I do not speak concerning all of you. I know whom I have chosen; and that the Scripture may be fulfilled, He (Judas) who eats bread with Me has lifted up his heal against Me. [54] Now I tell you before it comes, that when it does come to pass, you may believe that I am He. [55] Most assuredly, I say to you, "he/she who receives whoever I send receives Me." [56] When Jesus had said these things, He was troubled in Spirit, and testified and said, "Most assuredly, I say to you, one of you will betray Me."

[57] Then the Apostles looked at one another, perplexed about whom He spoke. [58] And there was leaning On Jesus bosom one of His Apostle, whom Jesus loved (Jesus' love everyone). [59] Simon Peter therefore motioned to Him to ask who it was who it was of whom He spoke. [60] Then leaning back on Jesus breast, he said to Him, "Lord, who is it." [46] Jesus answered, "It is he to whom I shall give a piece of bread when I have dipped it."

And having dipped the bread, He gave it to Judas Iscariot, the son of Simon. [61] Now after the piece of bread, Satan entered him. Then Jesus says to him, "What you do, do quickly." [62] And no one at the table knew for what reason He said that to him. [63] For some thought, because Judas had the money box, that Jesus had said to him, "Buy those things we need for the feast." Or that he should give something to the poor. [64] Having received the piece of bread, he then went out immediately, and it was night.

CHAPTER 35

1 Jesus weeps over Jerusalem

[1] Now as He draw near. He saw the city and wept over it, [2] saying, "Supposing you had known even you, especially is this your day, the things that make for your peace! And now they are hidden from your eyes. [3] For days will come upon you when your enemies will build an embarkment around you, surround you and close you in on every side, [4] and level you, and children within you, to the ground; and they will not leave in you one stone upon another, because you did not know the time of your visitation."

2 The destruction of Jerusalem

[5] And when you see Jerusalem surrounded by armies, then know that desolation is near. [6] Then let those who are in Judea flee to the mountains, let those who are in the midst of her heart, and let not those who are in the country enter her. [7] For these are the days of vengeance, that all things which are written may be fulfilled. [8] And woe to those who are pregnant and to those who are nursing babies in those days! For they will be great distress in the land and wrath upon this people. [9] And they will fall by the edge of the sword, and be led captive into all nations. And Jerusalem will be trample by Gentiles until the times of the Gentiles are fulfilled

3 The importance of watching

[10] "And take heed to yourselves, lest your hearts be weighed down with carousing drunkenness, and cares of this life, and that DAY come on you unexpectedly. [11] For it will come as a snare on all those who dwell on the face of the whole earth. [12] Watch therefore, and pray

always that you may be counted worthy to escape all these things that will come to pass, and to stand before the Son of Man." [13] And in the daytime, He was Teaching in the Temple, and at night He went out and stayed on the mountain called Olives. In the morning people came to Him in the Temple to hear Him.

4 The New Commandment

[14] So, when He had gone out, Jesus said, "Now the Son of Man is glorified, and God is glorified in Him. [15] When God is glorified in Him, God will also glorify Him in Himself, and glorify Him immediately. [16] Little Children, I shall be with you a little while longer. You will seek Me; and as I said to the Jews, where I am going, you cannot come; so now I say to you. [17] A new commandment I give to you, that you love one another; as I have loved you, that you also love one another. [18] By this all you know that you are My Disciples, when you have love for one another."

5 Jesus predict Peter denial

[19] Simon Peter said to Him, "Lord, where are You going?" Jesus answered him, "Where I am going you cannot follow Me now, and you shall follow Me afterward." [20] Peter said to Him, "Lord, why can I not follow You now? I will lay down my life for Your sake."

6 The WAY, the TRUTH, and the LIFE

[21] "Let not your heart be troubled; you believe in God, believe also in Me. [22] In My Father's house are many mansions, supposing it were not so, I would have not told you. I go to prepare a place for you. [23] And when I go and prepare a place for you, I will come again and receive you Myself; that where I am, there you may be also. [24] And where I go, you know, and the way you know." [25] Thomas said to Him, "Lord, we do not know where You are going, and how can we know the way?" [26] Jesus said to him, "I am the Way, the Truth and the Life. No one comes to the Father only through Me.

7 The Father revealed

[27] "Now that you know Me, you know My Father also, and from now on you know Him and have seen Him." [28] Philip says to him,

"Lord, show us the Father, and it is sufficient for us." [29] Jesus said to him, "Have I been with you so long, and yet you have not known Me, Philip? He who has seen Me has seen the Father? [30] Do you not believe that I am in the Father, and the Father in Me? The Words that I speak to you I do not speak on my own authority; and the Father who dwells in Me does the works. [31] Believe in Me that I am in the Father and the Father in Me, or else believe Me for the sake of the works themselves.

8 The answered prayer

[32] Most assuredly, I say to you, he/she who believes in Me, the works that I do he/she will do also; and greater works than these he/she will do, because I go to My Father. [33] And whatever you ask in My Name, that I will do, that the Father may be glorified in the Son. [34] When you ask anything in My Name, I will do it.

9 Jesus promised another Helper

[35] When you love Me, you keep my commandment. [36] And I will pray the Father, and He will give you another Helper---[37] The Spirit of Truth, Whom the world cannot receive, because it neither sees Him nor knows Him; except you know Him, for He dwells with you and will be in you. [38] I will not leave you orphans; I will come to you.

10 Indwelling of the Father and the Son

[39] "A little while longer and the world will see Me no more, and you will see me. Because I live, you will also live. [40] At that day you will know that I am in My Father, and you in Me, and I in you. [41] He/She who has My commandments and keeps them, it is he/she who loves Me. And he/she who loves Me will be loved by My Father, and I will love him/her and manifest to him/her."

[42] Judas (not Iscariot) said to Him, "Lord, how is it that You will manifest Yourself to us, and not to the world?" [43] Jesus answered and said to him, "When anyone loves Me, he/she will keep My Word; and My Father will love him/her, and we will come to him/her and make our home with him/her. [44] He/She who does not have Me does not keep My Words; and the Word which you hear is not Mine except it is the Father's Who sent Me.

11 The Gift of His Peace

[45] These things I have spoken to you while being present with you. [46] With the Helper, the Holy Spirit, Whom the Father will send in My Name, He will Teach you all things, and bring to your remembrance all things that I said to you. [47] Peace I live with you My Peace I give to you; not as the world gives do, I gave to you. Let not your heart be troubled, neither let it be afraid. [48] You have heard Me say to you, I am going away and coming back to you; because you love Me, you will rejoice because I am going to the Father; for My Father is greater than I. [49] And now I have told you before it comes, that when it does come to pass, you may believe. [50] I will no longer talk much with you, for the ruler of this world may know that I love the Father and as the father gave Me commandment, so I do. Arise, let us go from here.

12 The True Vine

[51] I am the True Vine, and My Father is the Vinedresser. [52] every Branch in Me that does not bear fruit He takes away, and every branch that bears fruit He prune, that it may bear more fruit, [53] You are already clean because of the Word which I have spoken to you. [54] Abide in Me, and I in you...... As the branch cannot bear fruit of itself, unless it abides in the Vine, neither can you, unless you abide in Me.

[55] I am the Vine you are the branches. He/She who abides in Me, and I in him/her, bears more fruit; for without Me you can do nothing. [56] When anyone does not abide in Me, he/she is cast as a branch and is withered; and they gather them and throw them into the fire, and they are burned. [57] When you abide in Me, and My Words abide in you, ask what you desire, and it shall be done for you. [58] By this My Father is glorified, that you bear much fruit; and you be my Disciples.

13 Love and joy perfected

[59] As the Father loved Me, I also loved you; abide in My love. [59] When you keep My commandments you will abide in My love, just as I have kept My Father's commandments and abide in His love. [60] These things that I have spoken to you, that My joy may remain in you, and that your joy may be full. [61] This is My commandment, that you love one another as I have loved you. [62] Greater loves have no one

than this, than to lay down one's life for his/her friends. [63] You are My Friends when you do whatever I command you. [64] No longer do I call you servants, for a servant does not know what is Master is doing; and I have call you friends, for all things that I heard from My Father I have made known to you.

[65] You did not choose Me, except I chose you and appointed you that you should go and bear fruit, and that your fruit should remain, that whatever you ask the Father in My Name He may give you. [66] these things I command you, that you love one another.

14 The world's hatred

[67] When the world hates you, you know that it hated Me before it hated you. [68] And supposing you were of the world, the world would love its own. Yet because you are not of the world, also, I chose you out of the world, therefore the world hates you. [69] Remember the word that I say to you, "A servant is not greater than his/her Master."

Because they persecute Me, they will also persecute you. When they will keep My Word, they will keep yours also. [70] And all these things they will do to you for My Name's sake, because they do not know Him Who sent Me. [71] And supposing I had not come and spoken to them, they would have no sin, except now they have no excuse for their sin.

[72] He who hates Me hates My Father also. [73] And supposing I had not done among them the works which no one else did, they would have no sin; except now they have seen and also hated both Me and My Father. [74] And this happened that the word might be fulfilled which is written in their Law, "They hated Me without a cause."

CHAPTER 36

1 The coming rejection

¹ And when the Helper come; Whom I shall send to you from the Father, the Spirit of Truth who proceeds from the Father, He will testify of Me. ² And you also will bear witness, because you have been with Me from the beginning. ³ these things I have spoken to you, that you should not be made to stumble. ⁴ They will put you out of the Synagogues; yes, then time is coming that whoever kills you will think that he offers God service. ⁵ And these things they will do to you because they have not known the Father nor Me. ⁶ And these things, I have told you, that when the time comes, you may remember that I told you of them. And these things I did not say to you at the beginning, because I was with you.

2 The work of the Holy Spirit

⁷ And now I go away to Him Who sent Me, and none of you ask, Me "Where You going?" ⁸ And because I have said these things to you, sorrow has filled your heart. ⁹ Nevertheless I tell you the truth. It is to your advantage that I go away, and supposing I do not go away, the Helper will not come to you; and when I depart, I will send Him to you. ¹⁰ And when He has come, He will convict the world of sin, and of righteousness, and of; judgment; ¹¹ of sin, because they did not believe in Me; ¹² of righteousness, because I go to My Father and you see Me no more, ¹³ of judgment, because the ruler of this world is judge. ¹⁴ I still have many things to say to you, and you cannot bear them now. ¹⁵ However, when He the Spirit of truth, has come, He will Guide you into all truth; for He will not speak on his own authority, what He will hear He will speak; and He will tell you things to come. ¹⁶ He will

glorify Me for He will take of what is Mine and declare it to you. [17] All things that the Father has are Mine. Therefore, I said that He will take of Mine and declare it to you.

3 Sorrow will turn to joy

[18] "A little while, and you will not see Me; and again, a little while, and you will see Me because I go to the Father." [19] Then some of the Apostles said among themselves, "What is this that He says to us, a little while, and you will not see Me; and again, a little while, and you will see me; and because I go to the Father."[20] They said therefore, "What is this that He says." [21] Now Jesus knew that they desired to ask Him, and He said to them, "Are you inquiring among yourselves about what I said, a little while, and you will not see Me; and again, a little while, and you will see Me? [22] Most assuredly, I say to you, that you will weep and lament, only the world will rejoice; and you will be sorrowful, and your sorrow will be turned into joy.

[23] A woman, who is in labor, has sorrow because her hour had come; and as soon she has given birth to the child, she no longer remembers the anguish, for joy that a human being has been born in the world. [24] Therefore you now have sorrow; and I will see you again and your heart will rejoice, and your joy no one will take from you. [25] And in that day, you will ask Me nothing. Most assuredly, I say to you, whatever you ask the Father in My Name He will give you. [26] Until now you have asked nothing in My Name. Ask, and you will receive, that your joy be full.

4 Jesus Christ has overcome the world

[27] These things I have spoken to you in figurative language; and the time is coming when I will no longer speak to you in figurative language, and I will tell you plainly about the Father." [28] I that day you will ask in My Name, and I do not say to you that I shall pray the Father for you; [29] for the Father Himself loves you, because you have loved Me, and have believed that I came forth from God. [30] I came forth from the Father and have come into the world. Again, I leave the world and go to the Father."

[31] His Apostles said to Him, "See, now you are speaking plainly, and using no figure of speech! Now we are sure that You know all

things, and have no need that anyone should question You. By this we believe that You came forth from God."

[33] Then Jesus answered them, "Do you not believe? [34] Indeed the hour is coming yes, has now comet hat you will be scattered, each to his own, and will leave Me alone. And yet I am not alone, because the Father is with Me. [35] These things, I have spoken to you, that in Me you may have peace. In the world you will have tribulation; and be of good cheer, I have overcome the world."

CHAPTER 37

1 Judas agrees to betray Jesus

¹ Then one of the twelve, Judas Iscariot, went to the Chief Priests ² and said, "What are you willing to give me to deliver Him to you?" And they counted to him thirty pieces of silver.

2 Jesus institutes the Lord supper

³ When the hour had come, He sat down, and the Apostles with Him. ⁴ Then He said to them, "With fervent desire, I have desired to eat this Passover with you before I suffer, ⁵ I will no longer eat of it until it is fulfilled in the Kingdom of God." ⁶ Then He took the cup, and gave thanks, and said, "Take this and divide it among yourselves; ⁷ from now on, I will not drink of the fruit of the vine until the Kingdom of God comes."

⁸ And He took bread, gave Thanks and break it, and gave it to them, saying, "This is My Body which is given for you; do this in remembrance of Me." ⁹ Likewise He also took the cup after supper, saying, "This cup is the New Covenant in My Blood, which I shed for you."

3 Jesus predicts Peter denial again

¹⁰ Then Jesus said to them, "All of you will be made to stumble because of Me this night, for it is written: I will strike the Shepherd, and the sheep will be scattered." (Zechariah 13:7). ¹¹ Peter said to Him, "Even when all are made to stumble, yet It will not be me." ¹² And the Lord said, "Simon, Simon! Indeed, Satan has asked for you, that he may sift you as a wheat. ¹³ And I have Pray for you, that your faith should not fail; and you have returned to Me, strengthen your brethren."

[14] "Assuredly, I say to you today, even this night, before the rooster crows, you will deny Me three times. [15] And he spoke more vehemently, "I will not deny You." And they all said likewise.

4 The prayer in the garden

[16] Then Jesus came with them to a place called Gethsemane, and said to the Apostles, "Sit here while I go pray over there." [17] And He took with Him Peter and the two sons of Zebedee, and He began to be sorrowful and deeply distressed. [18] Then He said to them, "My soul is exceedingly sorrowful, even to death. Stay here and watch with Me."

[19] He went a little farther and fell on His face, and prayed, saying, "O My Father, supposing it is possible, let this cup pass from Me; nevertheless, not as I will instead as Your will."

[20] Then He came to the Apostles and found them sleeping, and said to Peter, "what could you not watch with Me one hour? [21] Watch and pray, lest you enter into temptation. The spirit indeed is willing, only, the flesh is weak." [22] Again, a second time, He went away and prayed, saying, "O My Father, about this cup cannot pass away from Me unless I drink it, that Your will be done."

[23] And He came and found them asleep again, for their eyes were heavy. [24] So, He left them, went away again, and prayed the third time, saying, the same words. [25] Then He came to His Apostles and said to them, "Are you still sleeping and resting? Behold, the hour is at hand, and the Son of Man is being betrayed into the hands of sinners. [26] Rise let us be going. See, My betrayer is at hand."

5 Betrayal and arrest in Gethsemane

[27] And while He was still speaking, Behold, Judas, one of the twelve, with a great multitude with swords and clubs, came from the Chief Priests and elders of the people. [28] Now His betrayer had given them a sign, saying, "Whom ever I kiss, He is the One; seize Him." [29] Immediately he went up to Jesus and said, greeting, Rabbi!" And kissed Him. [30] And Jesus said to him, "Friend, why have you come?"

[31] Then they came and lays hands on Jesus and took Him. [32] And suddenly, one of those who were with Jesus stretched out his hand and drew his sword, struck the servant of the High Priest, and cut off

his ear. [33] And Jesus said to him, "Put your sword in its place, for all who take the sword will perish by the sword. [34] Or do you think that I cannot now pray to My Father, and He will provide Me with more than twelve legions of Angels? [35] How then could the Scriptures be fulfilled, that it must happen thus?"

[36] In that hour Jesus said to the multitudes, "Have you come out, as against a robber, with swords and clubs to take Me? I sat daily with you, Teaching in the Temple, and you did not seize Me. [37] And all this was done that the Scriptures of the Prophets might be fulfilled. And this is your hour, and the power of darkness."

CHAPTER 38

1 Before the High Priest

¹ And they led Jesus away to the High Priest; and with him were assembled all the Chief Priests, the elders, and the Scribes. ² And Peter followed Him at a distance, right into the courtyard of the High Priests. And he sat with the servants and warmed himself at the fire. ³ Now the Chief Priests and all the council sought testimony against Jesus to put Him to death, and found none.

⁴ For many bore false witness against Him, and their testimonies did not agree. ⁵ Then some rose up and bore false witness against Him, saying, ⁶ "We heard Him say, I will destroy this Temple made with hands, and within three days I will build another made without hands. ⁷ And even then, their testimony did not agree. ⁸ And the High Priests stood up in the midst and asked Jesus, saying, "Do You answered nothing? What is it these men testify against You?"

⁹ And He kept silent and answered nothing. Again, the High Priests asked Him, saying to Him, "Are You the Christ, the Son of the Blessed?" ¹⁰ Jesus said, "I am. And you will see the Son of Man sitting at the right hand of the Power, and coming with the clouds of Heaven."

¹¹ Then the High Priests tore his clothes and said, "What further need do we have of witnesses? ¹² You have heard the blasphemy! What do you think?" And they all condemned Him to be deserving of death. ¹³ Then some began to spit on Him, and to blindfold Him, and to beat Him, and say to Him, "Prophesy!" And the officers struck Him with the palms of their hands.

2 Peter denies Jesus and weep bitterly

[14] Having arrested Him, they led Him and brought Him into the High Priest's house. And Peter followed at a distance. [15] Now when they had kindled a fire in the midst of the courtyard and sat down together, Peter sat among them. [16] And a certain servant girl, seeing him as he sat by the fire, looked intently at him and said, "This man was also with Him." [17] And he denies Him, saying, "Woman I do not know Him." [18] And after a little while another saw him and said, "You also are of them." And Peter said, "I am not!"

[19] Then after about an hour had passed, another confidently affirmed, saying, "Surely thin fellow also was with Him, for he is a Galilean." [20] And peter said, "Man, I do not know what you are saying!" Immediately, while he was still speaking, a rooster crowed. [21] And the Lord turned and looked at Peter. Then Peter remembered the Word of the Lord, how He had said to him, "Before the rooster crows, you will deny Me three times." [22] So, Peter went out and wept bitterly.

3 Jesus handed over to Pontius Pilate

[23] When morning came, all the Chief Priests and elders of the people plotted against Jesus to put Him to death. [24] And when they had bound Him, they led Him away and delivered Him to Pilate the Governor. So early in the morning from Caiaphas house to the praetorium. And they themselves did not go into the praetorium, lest they should be defiled, and that they might eat the Passover. [25] Pilate then went out to them and said, "What accusation do you bring against this Man?" [26] They answered and said to him, "He is an evildoer, that's why we have Him delivered to you."

[27] Then Pilate said to them, "You take Him and judge Him according to your law." Therefore, the Jews says to him, "It is not lawful for us to put anyone to death." [28] That the saying of Jesus might be fulfilled which He spoke, signifying by what death He would die. [29] Then Pilate entered the praetorium again, called Jesus, and said to Him, "Are You the King of the Jews?" [30] Jesus answered him, "Are you speaking for yourself about this, or did others tell you this concerning Me?"

[31] Pilate answered, "Am I a Jew? Your own nation and the Chief Priests have delivered You to me. What have You done?" [32] Jesus

answered, "My kingdom is not of this world. Supposing My Kingdom were of this world, My servants would fight, so that I should not be delivered to the Jews; and now My kingdom is not from here."

33 Pilate therefore, said to Him, "Are You a King then?" Jesus answered, "you say rightly that I am a King. For this cause, I was born, and for this cause, I have come into the world, that I shall bear witness to the truth. Everyone who is of the truth hears My voice." 34 Pilate said to Him, "What is the truth?" And when he had said this, he went out again to the Jews, and said to them, "I find no fault in Him at all."

4 Jesus faces Herod

35 When Pilate heard, he asked is that Man a Galilean. 36 And as soon as he knew that He belonged to Herod's jurisdiction, he sent Him to Herod, who was also in Jerusalem at the time. 37 Now when Herod saw Jesus, he was exceedingly glad; for he has desired for a long time to see Him, because he had heard many things about Him, and he hoped to see some miracles done by Him.

38 Then he questioned Him with many words, and He answered him nothing. 39 And the Chief Priests and Scribes stood and vehemently accused Him. 40 Then Herod, with his men of war, treated Him with contempt and mocked Him, arrayed Him in a gorgeous robe, and sent Him back to Pilate. 41 That very day Pilate and Herod became friends with each other, for previously they had been at enmity with each other.

5 Judas hang himself

42 Then Judas His betrayer, seeing that he had been condemned, was remorseful and brought back the thirty pieces of silver to the Chief Priests and elders, saying, "I have sinned by betrayed innocent blood." And they say, "What is that to us? You see to it." 43 Then he threw down the pieces of silver in the Temple and departed, and went and hanged himself. 44 And the chief Priests took the silver pieces and said, "It is not lawful to put them in the treasury, because they are the price of blood."

45 And they consulted together and bought with them the Potter's field, to bury stranger in. 46 Therefore that field has been called the Field of Blood to this day. 47 Then was fulfilled what was spoken by Jeremiah the Prophet, saying, "and they took the thirty pieces of silver,

the value of Him who was "Priced", whom they the children of Israel priced, [48] and gave them for the Potter's field, as the Lord directed me."

6 Pilate decision

[49] Now at the feast the Governor was accustomed to releasing to the multitude, one prisoner whom they wished. [50] And at that time they had a notorious prisoner called Barabbas. [51] Therefore, when they had gathered together, Pilate said to them, "Whom do you want me to release to you? Barabbas or Jesus who is called Christ?" For he knew that they had handed Him over because of envy.

[52] While he was sitting on the judgment seat, his wife sent to him, saying, "Have nothing to do with that just Man, for I have suffered many things today in a dream because of Him." [53] And the Chief Priests and elders persuaded the multitude that they should ask for Barabbas and destroy Jesus. [54] The Governor answered and said to them, "Which of the two do you want me to release to you." They said, "Barabbas." [55] Pilate said to them, "What then shall I do with Jesus who is called Christ."

They said to him, "Let Him be crucified!" [56] Then the Governor said, "What evil has He done?" And they cried out all the more, saying, "Let Him to be crucified?!" [57] When Pilate saw that he could not prevail at all, and rather that a tumult was rising, he took water and washed his hands before the multitude, saying, "I am innocent of the blood of this person---you see to it." [58] And all the people answered and said, "His Blood be on us and our children." [59] Then he released Barabbas to them; and when he had scourged Jesus, he delivered Him to be crucified.

7 The soldiers mock Jesus

[60] Then the soldiers of the Governor took Jesus into the praetorium and gathered the whole garrison around Him. [61] And they stripped Him and put a scarlet robe on Him. [62] When they had twisted a crown of thorns, they put it on His head, and a reed in His right hand. And they bow the knee before Him and mocked Him, saying, "Hail King of the Jews?" [63] Then they spat on Him, and took the reed and struck Him on the head. [64] And when they had mocked Him, they took the robe off Him, put His own clothes on Him, and laid Him away to be crucified.

CHAPTER 39

1 The King on the cross

¹ Now as they led Him away, they laid hold of a certain man, Simon a Sirenian, who was coming into the country, and on him they laid the cross that he might bear it after Jesus. ² And a great multitude of the people followed Him, and women who also mourned and lamented Him. ³ And Jesus turning to them, said, "Daughters of Jerusalem, do not weep for Me, only weep for yourselves and for your children. ⁴ For indeed the days are coming in which they will say, "Blessed are the barren, womb's that never bore, and breasts which never nursed!"

⁵ Then they will begin to say to the mountains, "Fall on us!" And to the hills, "Covers us!" ⁶ For when they do these things in the green wood, "what we be done in the dry?" ⁷ And He bearing His cross, went out to a place called the place of a skull, which is called in Hebrew, Golgotha, ⁸ where they crucified Him and two others with Him, one on either side, and Jesus in the center. ⁹ Now Pilate wrote a title and put it on the cross. And the writing was---JESUS OF NAZARETH THE KING OF THE JEWS.

¹⁰ Then many of the Jews read this title, for the place where Jesus was crucified was near the city; and it was written in---Hebrew---Greek---and Latin--- ¹¹ Therefore, the Chief Priests of the Jews; said to Pilate, "Do not write, "The King of the Jews" instead write "I am the King of the Jews."

¹² Pilate answered, What I have written, I have written." They were also, two others who were robbers, to be put to death. ¹³ And one of the robbers said, "Suppose You are the Christ, save Yourselves and us." And the other answering, rebuked him, saying, "Do you not even fear God, seeing that you are under the same condemnation? ¹⁴ And we indeed

justly did receive the due reward of our deeds and this Man has done nothing wrong." ¹⁵ Then he said to Jesus, "Lord, remember me when You come into Your Kingdom." ¹⁶ And Jesus said to him, "Assuredly, I say to you, today you will be with Me in paradise."

¹⁷ And people were blaspheming Him, wagging their heads and saying, "Aha, You who destroy the Temple and build it after three days, ¹⁸ save Yourself and come down from the cross." ¹⁹ Likewise, the Chief Priests also mocking among themselves and the Scribes said, "He saved others; Himself He cannot save. ²⁰ Let the Christ, the King of Israel descend now from the cross, that we may see and believe." ²¹ Then the soldiers, when they had crucified Jesus, took His garments and made four parts, to each soldier a part, and also the tunic. Now the tunic was without seam, woven from the top in one piece. ²² They said therefore, among themselves, "Let us not tear it, only cast lots for it, whose it shall be." So, that the Scripture might be fulfilled which says: "They divide My garments among them, and for My clothing they cast lots."

2 Behold, Your mother

Now there stood by the cross of Jesus His mother, and His mother's sister, Mary the wife of Clopas, and Mary Magdalene. ²⁴ When Jesus therefore, saw His mother, and the Apostle whom He loved standing by, **(That Apostle John must love himself very, very much to almost every time he talked about himself a lot. And love it very much, for you to read that Jesus loved him, (maybe more than all the other Apostle) I got the impression that the Lord might remind him, later, that He love everyone the same.)** He said to His mother, "Woman Behold, your son!" ²⁵ Then He said to His Apostle "Behold, your mother!" And from that hour that Apostle took her to his own home.

3 Jesus died on the cross

²⁶ Now from the six hours until the ninth hour there were darkness over all the land. ²⁷ And about the ninth hour Jesus cried out with a loud voice, saying, "Eli, Eli, lama Sabathani?" That is "My God, My God why have You forsake Me?" ²⁸ Some of those who stood there, when they heard that, said, "This Man is calling for Elijah!" ²⁹ After this, Jesus knowing that all things were now accomplished, that the

Scripture might be fulfilled, said, I thirst!" ³⁰ Now a vessel full of sour wine was sitting there; and they filled a sponge with sour wine, put it on hyssop, and put it to His mouth. ³¹ So when Jesus had received the sour wine, He said, "It is finished." And bowing His head, He gave up His Spirit. ³² Then the veil of the Temple was torn in two from top to bottom; **(this is to tell us that the old ways just ended and a new covenant will be in force in, four days later.)** and the earth quaked, and the rocks were split. ³³ So when the centurion and those with him, who were guarding Jesus, saw the earthquake and the things that had happened, they feared greatly saying, "Truly this was the Son of God!"

4 Jesus side is pierced

³⁴ Because it was the Preparation Day, that the bodies should not remain on the cross on the Sabbath (And that Sabbath was a high day that year), the Jews asked Pilate that their legs might be broken, and that they might be taken away. ³⁵ Then the soldiers came and broke the legs of the first and to the other who was crucified with Him. ³⁶ And when they came to Jesus and saw that He was already dead, they did not break His legs. ³⁷ And one of the soldiers pierced His side with a spear, and immediately blood and water came out. ³⁸ And he who has seen has testified, and his testimony is true; and he knows that he is telling the truth, so that you may believe. ³⁹ For these things were done that the Scripture should be fulfilled.

"Not one of His bones be broken"

And again, another Scripture says,

"They shall look on Him Whom they pierced"

5 Jesus buried in Joseph's tomb

⁴⁰ Now when evening had come, because it was the Preparation Day, that is the day before the Sabbath, ⁴¹ Joseph of Arimathea, a prominent council member, who was himself waiting for the Kingdom of God, coming and taking courage, went in to Pilate and asked for the body of Jesus. ⁴² Pilate marveled that He was already dead and summoning the centurion, he asked him is He dead and when. So, when he found

out by the centurion, he granted the body to Joseph. [44] Then he bought fine linen, took Him down, and wrapped Him in the linen. And he laid Him in a tomb which had been hewn out of the rock, and rolled a stone against the door of the tomb. [45] And Mary Magdalene and Mary the mother of Joses observed where He was laid.

6 Pilate sets a guard

[46] On the next day, which followed the Day of Preparation, the Chief Priests and Pharisees gathered together to Pilate, saying, Sir, we remember, while He was still alive, how the deceiver said, "After three days I will rise!" [47] Therefore, command that the tomb be made secure until the fourth day, lest His disciples come by night and steal away, and say to the people, "He has risen from the dead! So, the last deception will be worse than the first." [48] Pilate said to them, "You have a guard; go your way, make it as secure as you know how." [49] So they went and made the tomb secure, sealing the stone and setting the guard.

7 He is risen

[50] Now after the Sabbath, as the first day of the week begin to dawn Mary Magdalene and the other Mary came to see the tomb. And Behold, for an Angel of the Lord descended from Heaven, and come and rolled back the stone from the door, and sat on it. [52] His countenance was like lightning, and his clothing as white as snow. [53] And the guard's sook for fear of him, and became like dead men. [54] And the Angel said to the women, "Do not be afraid, for I know that you seek Jesus who was crucified.

[55] He is not here for He is risen, as He said. Come, see the place were the Lord lay. [56] And go quickly and tell His Apostles that He is risen from the dead, and indeed He is going before you into Galilee; there you will see Him. Behold, I have told you." [57] So they went out quickly from the tomb with fear and great joy, and ran to bring His Apostles word.

8 The soldiers are bribe

[58] Now while they were going, Behold, some of the guards came into the city and reported to the Chief Priests all the things that had

happened. [59] When they had assembled with the elders and consulted together, they gave a large sum of money to the soldiers, [60] saying, "Tell, them His disciples came at night and stole Him when we were a slept. [61] And when this comes to the Governor's ears, we will appease him and make you secure." [62] So they took the money and did as they were instructed; and this saying is commonly reported among the Jews until this day.

CHAPTER 40

1 The road to Emmaus

¹ Now Behold, two of them were traveling that same day that Jesus was resurrected, to a village called Emmaus, which was seven miles from Jerusalem. ² And they talk together of all these things which had happened. ³ So it was, while they conversed and reasoned, that Jesus Himself drew near and went with them. ⁴ And their eyes were restrained, so that they did not know Him. ⁵ And He said to them, "What kind of conversation is this that you have with one another as you walk and are sad?" ⁶ And the one whose name was Cleopas answered and said to Him, "Are You the only stranger in Jerusalem, and have You not know the things which happened there in these days?" ⁷ And He said to them, "What things?" And they said to Him, "These things concerning Jesus of Nazareth who was a Prophet mighty in deed and Word before God and all the people, ⁸ and how the Chief Priests and our rulers delivered Him to be condemned to death, and crucified Him. ⁹ And we were hoping that it was He Who was going to redeemed Israel. Indeed, besides all this, today is the fourth day since these things happened. ¹⁰ Yes, and certain women of our company, who arrived at the tomb early, astonished us. ¹¹ When they did not find His body, they came saying that they had seen a vision of an Angel who said He was alive. ¹² And certain of those who were with us went to the tomb and fond it just as the women had said; and Him they did not see."

2 The Disciples eyes opened

¹³ Then they drew near to the village where they were going, ¹⁴ and they constrained Him, saying, "Abide with us, for it is toward evening, and the day is far spent." And He went in to stay with them. ¹⁵ Now it

came to pass, as He sat at the table with them, that He took the bread, blessed and broke it, and gave it to them. [16] then their eyes were opened and they knew Him. [17] Then He said to them, "O, foolish one, and slow of heart to believe in all that the Prophets have spoken![18] Ought not the Christ to have suffered these things and to enter into His glory?" [19] And beginning at Moses and all the Prophets, He expounded to them in all the Scriptures the things concerning Himself. And He vanished from their sight.

[20] And they said to one another, "Did not our heart burn within us while He talked with us on the road, and while He opened the Scriptures to us?" [21] So they rose up that very hour and returned to Jerusalem, and found the eleven and those who were with them gathered together, [22] saying, "The Lord is risen indeed, and has appeared to Simon?!" [23] And they talked about these things that had happened on the road, and how He was know to them in the breaking of bread.

3 Jesus appeared to His Apostles

[24] Now as they said these things, Jesus Himself stood in the midst of them, (the ten Apostles, Thomas was absent) and said to them, "Peace to you." [25] And they were terrified and frightened, and supposed they had seen a spirit. [26] And He said to them? "Why are you troubled? And why do doubts arise in your heart? [27] Behold My hands and feet, that it is I Myself. Handle Me and see, for a spirit does not have flesh and bones as you see I have." [28] When He had said this, He showed them His hands and His feet. And while they still did not believe for joy, and marveled, He said to them, "have you any food here?" [29] So they gave Him a piece of broiled fish and some honeycomb. [30] And He took it and eat in their presence.

4 Seeing and Believing

[31] Now Thomas, called the twin, one of the twelve, was not with them when Jesus came. [32] The other Apostles therefore said to Him, "We have seen the Lord." And he said to them, "Unless I see in His hands the print of the nails, and put my finger into the print of the nails, and put my hand into His side, I will not believe." [33] And after eight days His Apostles were again inside, and Thomas with them. Jesus came, the doors being shut, and stood in the midst, and said, "Peace to

you!" [34] Then He said to Thomas, "Reach your finger here, and look at My hands; and reach your hand here, and put it into My side. Do not be unbelieving, instead believing."

[35] And Thomas answered and said to Him, "My Lord and My God!" Jesus said to him, "Thomas, because you have seen Me, you have believed. Blessed he/she who have not seen and yet have believed."

5 Jesus prays for Himself

[36] Jesus spoke these words, lifted up His eyes to Heaven, and said: "Father, the Hour has come. Glorify Your Son, that Your Son also may glorify You, [37] as You have given Him Authority over all flesh, that He shall give Eternal Life to as many as You have given Him. [38] And this is Eternal Life, that they may know You, the only True God and Jesus Christ whom You have sent. [39] I have glorified You on the earth. I have finished the work which You have given Me to do. [40] And now, O Father, glorify Me together with Yourself, with the glory which I had with You before the world was.

6 Jesus prays for His Apostles

[41] I have manifested Your Name to the men whom You have given Me out of the world. They were Yours, You, gave them to Me, and they have kept Your Word. [42] Now they have known that all things which You have given Me are from You. [43] For I have given to them the words which You have given Me; and they have received them, and have known surely that I came forth from You; and they have believed that You sent Me.

[44] I pray for them. I do not pray for the world and for those whom You have given Me, for they are Yours. [45] And all Mine are Yours, and Yours are Mine, and I am glorified in them. [46] Now I am no longer in the world and I come to You. Holy Father, keep through Your Name, those whom You have given Me, that they may be one as we are. [47] while I was with them in the world, I kept them in Your Name. Those whom You gave Me I have Kept; and none of them is lost except the son of perdition, that the Scripture might be fulfilled. [48] And now I come to You, and these things I speak in the world, that they may have My joy fulfilled in themselves.

⁴⁹ I have given them Your Word; and the world has hated them because they are not of the world, just as I am not of the world. ⁵⁰ I do not pray that You should take them out of the world, and that You should keep them from the evil one. ⁵¹ They are not of the world, just as I am not of the world. ⁵² Sanctify them by Your Truth. Your Word is Truth. As You sent Me into the world, I also sent them into the world. ⁵⁴ And for their sakes I Sanctify Myself, that they also may be sanctified by the Truth.

7 Jesus prays for all believers

⁵⁵ I do not pray for these alone, and also for those who will believe in Me through their word; ⁵⁶ that they all may be one, as You Father, are in Me, and I in You; that they also may be one of us, that the world may believe that You sent Me. ⁵⁷ And the glory which You give Me I have given them, that they may be one just as we are one: ⁵⁸ I in them, and You in Me; that they may be made perfect in one, and that the world may know that You have sent Me, and have loved them as You have loved Me. ⁵⁹ Father, I desire that they also whom You gave Me may be with Me where I am, that they may behold My glory which You have given Me; for You loved Me before the foundation of the world.

⁶⁰ O righteous Father! The world has not known You, like I have known You; and these have known that You sent Me. ⁶¹ And I have declared to them Your Name, and will declare it, that the love which You loved Me may be in them, and I in them."

CHAPTER 41

<u>1 Breakfast by the sea</u>

[1] After these things Jesus showed Himself again to the Apostles at the sea of Tiberias, and in the way He showed Himself: [2] Simon Peter, Thomas called the twin, Nathanael of Cana in Galilee, the sons of Zebedee and two others of His Apostles were together. [3] Simon Peter said to them "I am going fishing." They said to him "We are going with you also." They went out and got into the boat, and that night they caught nothing. [4] And when the morning had now come, Jesus stood on the shore; yet the Apostles did not know that it was Jesus. [5] Then Jesus said to them, "Children, have you any food?" They answered Him "No." [6] And He said to them, "Cast the net on the right side of the boat, and you will find some." So, they cast, and now they were not able to draw it because of the multitude of fish.

[7] Therefore, that apostle that Jesus loved (that john he really loved himself) said to Peter, "It is the Lord!" Now when Simon Peter heard that it was the Lord, he put on his outer garment and plunged into the sea. [8] And the other Apostles came in the little boat, dragging the net wish fish. [9] Then, as soon as they had come to land, they saw a fire of coals there, and fish laid on it, and bread. [10] Jesus said to them, "Bring some of the fish which you have just caught."

[11] Simon Peter went up and dragged the net to land, full of large fish, one hundred and fifty--three; and although there were so many, the net was not broken. [12] Jesus said to them, "Come and eat breakfast." Yet none of the Apostles dared ask Him, "Who are You?" ---Knowing that it was the Lord. [13] Jesus then came and took the bread and gave it to them, and likewise the fish. [14] This is now the third time Jesus showed Himself to His Apostles after He was raised from the dead.

2 Jesus restore Peter

[15] So when they had eaten breakfast, Jesus said to Simon Peter, "Simon, son of Jonah, do you love Me more than these?" He said to Him, "Yes, Lord; You know that I love You." He said to him, "Feed My Lambs." [16] He said to him again a second time, "Simon, son of Jonah, do you love Me." He said to Him, "Yes, Lord, You know that I love You." He said to him, "Tend My sheep." [17] He said to him the third, Simon, son of Jonah, do you love Me." And he said to Him, "Lord You know all things; You know that I love You." Jesus said to him, "Feed My sheep. [18] Most assuredly, I say to you, when you were younger, you girded yourself and walked where you wished; and where your old, you will stretch out your hands, and another will gird you and carry you where you do not wish." [19] This He spoke, signifying by what dead he will glorify God. And when He had spoken this, He said to him, "Follow Me."

3 The Scriptures Opened

[20] Then He said to them, "these are the Words which I spoke to you while I was still with you, that all things must be fulfilled which were written in the Law of Moses and the Prophets and the Psalms concerning Me." [21] And He opened their understanding, that they might comprehend the Scriptures. [22] Then He said to them, "This it is written, and thus it was necessary for the Christ to suffer and to rise from the dead the fourth day, [23] and that repentance and remission of sins should be preached in His Name to all nations, beginning at Jerusalem. [24] And you are witnesses of these things. [25] Behold, I send the promise of My Father upon you; and tarry (meaning: to be delay) in the city of Jerusalem until you are endued with "Power" from on High."

4 The ascension

[26] And He led them out as far as Bethany, and He lifted up His hands and blessed them. [27] Now it came to pass, while He blessed them, that He was parted from them and carried up into Heaven. [28] And they worshiped Him, and returned to Jerusalem with great joy, [29] and were continually in the Temple praising and blessed God.

<u>5 That you may believe</u>

And truly Jesus did many other signs in the presence of His Disciples and His Apostles, which are not written in this book. (This John talking about his Gospel and it was most likely Papyrus paper written on and it was not actually a book, yet, later, yes. So it is not about the Bible that John talk about, because the Real Bible as we know now didn't came, many, many, years). ---And these are written that you believe that Jesus is the Christ, the Son of God, and that believing you may have life in His Name. Amen.

HAPPY READING. -----NORM.